Angelókastro The medieval fortress offers sweeping views *(page 71)*

Listón Kérkyra Town's elegant promenade was modelled on the Rue de Rivoli in Paris *(page 33)*

Byzantine Museum A fine collection of icons and religious artefacts, housed in a 15th-century church *(page 36)*

Museum of Asian Art Unexpected, world-class collection in Kérkyra Town *(page 31)*

Archaeological Museum The massive Gorgon pediment dominates this Kérkyra Town attraction *(page 43)*

The west coast Noted for its glorious sandy beaches, including Glyfáda and Kondogialós *(page 72)*

A PERFECT WEEK

Day 1 — Corfu Town

Start with coffee at venerable Zizimos café on the Listón. Cross the Spianáda to take in the Paleó Froúrio in the morning light, then marvel at the Asian Art Museum. After lunch, climb the Néo Froúrio for the views, then head out to Glyfáda or Kondogialós for a swim before watching the sunset from the Kaiser's Throne. Return to town for some late shopping and dinner.

Day 2 — The South

Head south via the Paleópolis museum, then visit the Achilleion. Lunch at a Boúkari seafood taverna, then spend the afternoon at one of the fine beaches of the southwest coast. Try Klimataria (see page 108) in Benítses for supper.

Day 3 — Northeast

Head northeast, pausing at the National Gallery Annexe or the Byzantine church in Ágios Márkos. Lunch is along the 'Kensington on Sea' coast. Kalámi has the best pebble beach hereabouts, but you might rent a boat to seek out your own secluded cove. Later, drive up to Paleá Períthia to dine on the old village square. Change your overnight base to Róda or Aharávi.

Day 4 — Eríkoussa

Board a morning excursion boat in Róda or Sidári for a day trip to Eríkoussa, sandiest and closest of the Diapóndia islets. On your return, head to Perouládes to watch the sunset from the cliffs over Longás beach. Have supper at Kohili (see page 111) in Ágios Stéfanos Gýrou, or, for simpler taste, the Xenykhtis grill (see page 112) in Afiónas village.

IN CORFU

Vório

Nisí Vídos

Páxos (Gaíos), Igoumenítsa, Pátra, Kefaloniá

Day 6 Paxí and Andípaxi

Take a day cruise to these two islets south of Corfu. Likely targets will be the Paxiot west coast with its spectacular Orthólithos stack and sea caves, or the mock-Caribbean coves of Vríka and Vatoúmi on Andípaxi. Dinner on return in Kérkyra Town – perhaps La Famiglia (see page 106) for some Italian fare.

Day 5 Northwest

Start the day at magnificent Ágios Geórgios Págon beach, then reach the castle of Angelókastro before afternoon closure. Lunch is at Lákones for its views over Paleokastrítsa, your late-afternoon destination – perhaps another swim before visiting the lovely Theotókou monastery towards dusk. Have dinner in Doukádes village, at Elizabeth's (see page 112).

Day 7 Round-up

Today, catch whatever you've missed so far. Say the Archaeological Museum in town, with its imposing Gorgon pediment; the outstanding icon collection inside the Byzantine Museum; or the Folklore Museum in Sinarádes. Have lunch at the little seaview taverna above Myrtiótissa beach, and after a swim gain entrance to the historic monastery here.

CONTENTS

60

33

61

83

Features

79

95

INTRODUCTION

Swathed in a blanket of deep green, its mountainous skyline plunging into a crystal-clear, turquoise sea, Corfu is known as Greece's Emerald Island. It is not only among the lushest of Greece's myriad islands but one of the prettiest as well. Flowering bushes, shrubs and trees cloak most of its rolling landscape, and in spring the island is bursting with beautiful wild flowers.

Corfu's sunny beaches, spectacular scenery and charming capital have enchanted visitors – including many writers and artists – throughout the centuries. The wonderful clear light and stunning vistas of the island are thought to have been the inspiration for settings in Homer's *Odyssey* and Shakespeare's *Tempest*. In more recent times, the British writer and painter Edward Lear depicted many views of Corfu's now famous sights, while the authors Lawrence and Gerald Durrell both lived here and wrote entertaining books about island life. Many celebrities and industrial magnates, from the Rothschilds and the Agnellis (of Fiat fame) to the Greek royal family and the empress of Austria, have had villas built on the island.

Secluded Resorts

Since the late 1970s, Corfu has become a popular British playground; for many years over half of all the island's holiday visitors came from the UK. No doubt early visitors felt very much at home sipping ginger beer and watching cricket matches in Kérkyra Town (Corfu Town) – both relics of British rule (1814–64) that can still be enjoyed today. The introduction of cheap package tourism in the 1980s gave Corfu something

The dramatic beauty of the northeast coast

All Greek to me

Language is no problem for most visitors. Many locals speak English or Italian, and most signs are posted in both Greek and Roman characters.

of a reputation as a 'party island'. However, the party scene was always restricted to a few enclaves, and since the millennium some of those have mellowed considerably. Nonetheless, there are definitely still a few places that are best avoided by anyone who prefers the atmosphere of a Greek island to a rowdy British seaside town. Lately, however, numbers of central/eastern Europeans – Poles, Serbs, Russians, Czechs, Romanians and Bulgarians – have risen sharply.

In keeping with island character and scale, many resorts are small, quiet and secluded. Though development has been rapid on some parts of Corfu, it is still much less overbearing than in many other Mediterranean vacation destinations. In marked contrast to the European mainland, there are no high-rise horrors and only the occasional large hotel. Actually, much of the island remains untouched by mass tourism, and the main resorts are really crowded only in July and August. Remarkably, even in peak season you can still find secluded places for sunbathing and hiking along the coastline and throughout the hilly hinterland. You just have to make an extra effort (usually either on foot or by boat) to get there.

Location and Size

Corfu is the most northerly of the Ionian group of islands. Just across the water to the east are Albania and the Greek mainland. Italy lies only 40 nautical miles to the northwest. To the south are delightful Paxí and the other Ionian islands (Lefkáda, Itháki, Kefaloniá, Zákynthos and Kýthira); however, island-hopping is an option only for travellers with lots of time on their hands.

Corfu is also Greece's western gateway and has proudly styled itself 'the entry to the Adriatic'. It is telling that the Ottomans – who conquered the rest of mainland Greece and Lefkáda among the Ionian islands – failed to gain a foothold here. Instead, it was the great Western European powers of the day (Venice, France and Britain) who left their mark during five centuries of island occupation. Nowhere is this more noticeable than in the elegant architecture and cosmopolitan atmosphere of Kérkyra Town. Where else in the world could you sit at a French-style café, amid Venetian streets, sipping Greek coffee while gazing at an English palace? This stylish capital is regarded as the loveliest town in all the Greek islands, and a visit here is a highlight of most visitors' holidays.

In its shape Corfu resembles a scythe, measuring about 65km (40 miles) in length and ranging in width from 4km to 30km (2.5 miles to 19 miles). According to geologists, the

The Listón, Kérkyra (Corfu) Town

island is the exposed crown of a submerged mountain range that broke off eons ago from the mainland to the east. The highest point is Mt Pandokrátor, really only a fairly modest-sized peak of 914m (2,970ft). But on this relatively small island it takes on much more importance, and the summit is approached by an impressive ascent along steep hairpin bends.

Hire a car, if only for a few days. No matter where you are based, you can very easily get around and explore the whole island. As you tour Corfu you'll see on the undulating hills and stone-hedged terraces silvery groves of prized olive trees – venerable and gnarled. In the past they were an economic lifeline for the island, and they still provide excellent olive oil, and wood for carving souvenirs. The island is also graced with legions of kumquat and lemon trees (giving off a glorious aroma in spring), plane trees, jacaranda, palms, wisteria, myrtle and oleander. Even the simplest homes are adorned with verdant grape arbours and enormous, beautiful clusters of roses or bougainvillea. Most memorable of all are the groves of tall, slim cypresses rising like sentries on the hillsides.

Visit in spring or early summer if possible to see the best of the island's flora: there are 100 native wild flowers alone that grow nowhere else. You might get a little wet then, but it's a price worth paying. The reason for Corfu's remarkably luxuriant vegetation is that more rain falls here – deflected by the nearby mainland mountains – than in any other part of Greece. However, for most of the year this is very much an island in the sun.

Clean Beaches, Casual Living

Corfu has about 200km (125 miles) of coastline with some of Europe's most beautiful and cleanest beaches. They vary from strips of pure golden sand to fine pea-gravel to bright white pebbles, or combinations of all three. While swells for surfing can be found on the western shores, there are plenty of calm bays suitable for all the family on the more protected east coast. As for the sea itself, in any one cove the range of clear blues seems to defy the colour spectrum. Don't miss a day trip to the Diapóndia islets or Andípaxi, where the waters are as clear as those in the Caribbean.

Around 113,000 people live on Corfu. Some emigrate – attracted by life abroad or in the big mainland cities – but countless others have never left the island. Instead, the world comes to them, in increasing numbers that today reach one mil-

The Catholic Cathedral

lion annually. Yet despite the seasonal influx of visitors, the inhabitants on the whole retain a fresh, open simplicity that delights visitors.

Life on Corfu is casual and unhurried. For the punctilious northern European visitor it can sometimes be a bit too casual: waiting for a bus that is 20 minutes late (or never comes); the 'fast-food' *souvláki* for which you have to queue for 15 minutes; the restaurant order that takes an eternity, then arrives cold. Be patient and remember that nobody ever came to Corfu (or anywhere else in Greece, for that matter) for swift service, gourmet French food or impeccable plumbing. After all, the slow pace of life here is intrinsic to *filoxenía* (traditional Greek hospitality to strangers).

A BRIEF HISTORY

Little is known about Corfu's first inhabitants. Prehistoric traces found at Gardíki in the southwest date back to the Middle Palaeolithic Era (c.40,000BC), when the island was probably joined to the Greek mainland. But unlike on other Ionian islands, no traces of Mycenaean settlements have ever surfaced on Corfu, which may instead have been held by the Phoenicians during the late Bronze Age (1500BC to 1150BC).

Corfu's acknowledged history begins in 734BC, when the Corinthians established a colony called Korkyra south of today's Kérkyra Town in an area known as Paleópolis (Old City). Archaeological digs (still in progress) have

Ulysses and the Stone Ship

According to Homer's *Odyssey*, the hero Ulysses ('Odysseus' in Greek) was shipwrecked during his 10-year voyage home from the Trojan War. He was washed ashore on the island of Skheria – the ancient name of Corfu – which was inhabited by the Phaeacians. There he was found by Princess Nausikaa and her handmaidens when they came to wash clothes at a nearby stream. She persuaded her father, King Alkinoös, to provide a boat to return him to his native Ithaca, but this assistance angered Poseidon (the god of the sea), who turned the ship to stone in revenge for Odysseus' killing of the Cyclops, a son of Poseidon.

Three Corfu sites claim to be the Homeric place where Ulysses' boat was petrified. All have the requisite double harbour approached by a narrow causeway, as well as an offshore rock that (with a bit of imagination) resembles a petrified ship. These are Mouse Island, off Kanóni; Kolóvri, south of Paleokastrítsa; and Krávia (meaning 'ship'), northwest of Cape Arílla. The beach where Ulysses was washed ashore is touted as the west coast's Érmones, largely on account of its small stream.

turned up temples near Kardáki Spring and Mon Repos, but the ancient city was otherwise destroyed by barbarian raiders, its stone masonry subsequently used to build medieval Kérkyra Town. The famous 6th-century BC Gorgon pediment from the Temple of Artemis, now in the Archaeological Museum, is the most important surviving artefact of classical Korkyra.

Odysseus and Nausikaa depicted by Allesandro Allori

Prospering from trade with southern Italy, Korkyra grew into a strong maritime power. In 665BC, Korkyra defeated Corinth in what the historian Thucydides described as the first naval battle in Greek history, thus gaining independence and subsequently founding colonies of her own. Corfu's pact with Athens against Corinth and Sparta in 433BC proved to be, according to Thucydides, the final straw that set off the Peloponnesian War and hastened the end of classical Greece.

From then on, Corfu suffered attack, pillage and often highly destructive occupation. Situated barely a nautical mile from the Epirot mainland at its nearest point, Corfu's safe harbours, fertile soil and strategic position between the Adriatic and Ionian seas made it a prize worth contesting by any power aiming to control the region.

Roman Conquest, Barbarian Raids

Around 229BC a Roman fleet arrived and seized the island from the Illyrians, making Corfu the Roman republic's earliest Adriatic conquest. For the next five and a half centuries,

Corfu prospered as a Roman naval base. En route to and from battles – or simply as tourists – Nero, Tiberius, Cato, Cicero, Caesar, Octavian and Mark Antony (with Cleopatra) were among the Roman notables who visited Corfu. During the 1st century AD two saints – Iason (Jason) and Sosipatros (Sosipater) – brought Christianity to the island. Certain structures at Paleópolis are among the few remnants from Corfu's Roman period.

When the Roman Empire split in the 4th century AD, its eastern half, Byzantium, took administrative control of Corfu but could provide little security. Rampaging Vandals raided the island in 445, while in 562 a horde of Ostrogoths badly damaged Corfu's ancient capital which, however, was only slowly abandoned from the 7th century on.

Partway through the 10th century, the Corfiots moved their capital 2km (1 mile) north and built their first fortress on the rocky bluff commanding the town's eastern sea approach. The Old Fort still stands today on this site. Elsewhere, islanders abandoned coastal settlements and retreated inland to establish protected hillside villages.

Normans and Sicilians

Then appeared a formidable new enemy. Several times between 1080 and 1185, Norman forces crossed the sea from Sicily and Italy to attack Corfu and nearby outposts of the enfeebled Byzantine Empire. The rulers in Constantinople asked for help, the Venetians responded and thereafter took an active interest in the destiny of both Corfu and the empire as a whole.

When Doge Enrico Dandolo and his Fourth Crusade seized Constantinople in 1204, the spoils claimed by Venice included western Greece, parts of the Peloponnese, and the Ionian islands. But Venice was unable to extend immediate control over all its new possessions, and Corfu aligned itself with the Greek Despotate of Epirus, which then held parts of what are today Albania and western Greece. In 1214 Mikhaïl Angelos Komnenos II, head of the despotate, formally acquired the island, strengthening existing fortresses at Angelókastro and Gardíki.

However, the Normans still had designs on Corfu. In 1259, the island was presented to King Manfred, the Hohenstaufen king of Sicily, as Mikhaïl's daughter Helena's dowry. Eight years later, the new king of Sicily and Naples, Charles d'Anjou, became the overlord of Corfu, where his family – the Angevins – subsequently ruled for over a century. During this time the traditional Eastern Orthodoxy of the island was almost extinguished by the new official religion of Roman Catholicism.

Venetian Rule

As Angevin power diminished, Corfu's fledgling assembly of 24 barons, mindful of the danger presented by marauding corsairs, invited Venice to send in a protective military force. The Venetians landed on 20 May 1386, beginning an uninterrupted

A relic of Byzantine rule: the church of Ágii Iáson and Sosípatros

Corfu's Old Fort

occupation that lasted for over four centuries. In the following year, Corfu officially became part of the Stato da Màr, the Venetian maritime empire. Kérkyra Town prospered once again as a key port for galleys plying far-flung commercial routes, and the Venetians turned the Byzantine fort in Kérkyra Town into an impregnable bastion.

In 1463, having swept across mainland Greece, the Ottoman Turks declared war on Venice. During the following years they mounted many assaults on the Ionian Islands, and in 1537 they turned on Corfu. Intent on seizing Kérkyra Town, the Ottoman fleet, led by pirate-admiral Hayreddin Barbarossa, a Greek renegade from Lésvos, landed cannon and 25,000 troops north of the capital at Gouviá. The fortress withstood a bitter attack, but the rest of the island was looted and the vengeful Turks carried off some 15,000 to 20,000 prisoners – nearly half the population – into slavery.

Following this great siege, the Venetians dug the Contrafossa, a canal separating the Old Fort from the town. They also erected a 'New Fortress' (so called even today) to guard the city's northwestern approach.

Corfu's finest military hour was to come in July 1716, once more against the Turks and once more at great cost. After losing both Athens and the Peloponnese to the Venetians late in the 17th century, the Ottomans successfully counterattacked, retaking the Peloponnese and Lefkáda before sending over 30,000 troops to besiege Corfu. Venice hired foreign regiments under the German mercenary commander Johann Matthias von der Schulenburg to defend the island. For five bloody weeks just 8,000 defenders held Kérkyra Town while the Turks, with their overwhelmingly superior forces, ravaged the rest of the island. They appeared poised to capture the capital when they suddenly called off their assault and fled, after severe casualties occasioned by a ferocious storm in August. The Ottomans never returned, and Corfu (along with all the other Ionian isles, save Lefkáda) was the only part of Greece never to be subjugated by the Ottomans.

Throughout its long occupation, Venice kept Corfu under a strict feudal regime, a colony valued as an important naval base, trading depot and tariff-collection station. A civil-military governor and senior bureaucrats sent from Venice ran the island. Much like Venice's Libro d'Oro, a Golden Book listing the Corfiot nobility contained 277 families at the time that Corfu passed from Venetian hands to Napoleonic forces.

However, ordinary islanders were heavily taxed and denied public education, and Greek Orthodoxy was eclipsed by Roman Catholicism. Italian replaced Greek as the official language, even though the peasantry couldn't understand it and had no way of learning it. Many laboured as serfs in the Venetian aristocrats' villas, some of which still dot the countryside.

More happily, Venice was responsible for nearly all the olive trees that grace Corfu's landscape. Eager to ensure

Patron saint

It is said that at the height of the Ottoman siege of August 1716, St Spyridon appeared amidst a raging storm with a lighted torch and scared the invaders away. August 11 is now one of the days that commemorate Corfu's patron saint (see page 39).

Corfu became part of
Napoleon's empire

a constant supply of oil, the republic at one stage decreed a cash bonus for every 100 trees planted. Olive production transformed the island's economy for good. Apart from the olive trees, the most visible legacy of Venetian rule are the older districts of Kérkyra Town: with its narrow streets and tall buildings, it is the most European city in Greece.

Napoleon's Dream Island

In 1797 the doges' republic and its possessions fell to Napoleon through the Treaty of Campo Formio, thus ending 411 years of Venetian occupation. For reasons that remain obscure, Napoleon was rather obsessed with Corfu. 'The greatest misfortune which could befall me is the loss of Corfu,' he wrote rather melodramatically to his foreign minister, Talleyrand, and quickly sent a force to occupy Corfu and the other Ionian Islands.

Napoleonic forces replaced Venice's autocratic rule with new democratic representation, burned Corfu's Golden Book, introduced public education and made Greek the official language. Nevertheless, they still managed to antagonise the island's inhabitants by continuing to suppress the Orthodox Church. Within two years the French were driven out of the island by a joint Russo-Turkish force that reinstated Greek Orthodoxy as the official religion under the puppet 'Septinsular Republic'. However, in 1807 the French regained Corfu from the Russians by the Treaty of Tilsit. This time Napoleon garrisoned the citadels with 50,000 men along with

500 new cannon, making Corfu one of the most powerfully fortified points in the eastern Mediterranean.

The French also established the first Ionian Academy for the promotion of arts and sciences, imported Greece's first printing presses, drew up a street plan for Corfu Town, built a miniature Rue de Rivoli (the Listón) and introduced the cultivation of potatoes and tomatoes, now mainstays of Corfiot cooking.

The British Move In

After Napoleon's defeat at Waterloo, the British took Corfu in 1814 by the terms of the Treaty of Vienna, which turned the seven Ionian Islands into a notional state under British 'protection'. Corfu became the capital and Sir Thomas Maitland was appointed the first Lord High Commissioner.

The British occupation of Corfu lasted for just 50 years, and brought certain benefits. Under Maitland, a road network

The First European

Corfu's most famous son is Ioannis Kapodistrias (1776–1831). Born into an aristocratic family, he became Greece's first president in 1827 and is hailed as the first statesman to envisage a unified Europe. From 1799 until 1807, Kapodistrias was instrumental in the administration of the Septinsular Republic under Russian tutelage. He then served until 1822 as a diplomat in the Russian court of Tsar Alexander I. On a mission to Switzerland in 1813, he orchestrated the Swiss Federation, which has remained in place to this day. In the ensuing years he began to develop ideas of a unified Europe in which no one member would become too powerful and in which the powers would collectively regulate the whole. In this vision he was a man ahead of his time. Sadly, his political ideals also brought him parochial enemies, and he was assassinated on the Greek mainland in 1831 by two clan chieftains. In 1994 his home island fittingly hosted a summit meeting of the very union of which he had dreamed.

was built. His successor, Frederick Adam, built the road to Paleokastrítsa and brought a permanent water-supply system to Kérkyra Town. While some changes were mere personal caprice on the part of the ten British high commissioners, they also introduced hospitals, a model prison, a decent judiciary, and religious freedom, ensuring the primacy of the Orthodox Church. The slightly eccentric Frederic North, 5th Earl of Guilford – a philhellene who went about in Classical Greek dress, and actually converted to Orthodox Christianity – established modern Greece's first university, the second Ionian Academy, in Kérkyra Town in 1824. He bequeathed to it his library of 25,000 books and helped to make Corfu the country's chief literary and intellectual centre of its day.

The constitution set in place by Maitland was another matter. Though maintaining a façade of parliamentary government with a Corfiot senate and assembly, the high commissioner retained all effective power. Serious unrest first occurred in the 1820s, when Maitland stopped the Corfiots from giving assistance to Greek mainlanders engaged in the war of independence against Turkey. This engendered bitterness among the islanders, who dubbed Maitland 'the abortion' for his rudeness, and aversion to bathing.

As a strong movement for unification with the mainland arose after Greece emerged as a state in 1830, the British introduced token constitutional reforms (unrestricted press and liberalised election procedures), but the high commissioner's power remained intact. However, agitation for union – énosis – continued to grow.

The British legacy

The British left behind a number of stately buildings and monuments as well as cricket, ginger beer and Christmas chutney – island favourites even today.

Greek at Last

When Prince William of Denmark was crowned King George I in Athens in 1864,

Corfu and the six other Ionian Islands were ceded to Greece as a condition of George's accession to the throne. The islands were declared 'perpetually neutral', and, before hauling down the Union Jack, the British blew up the impressive fortifications they had added to Kérkyra Town. When they sailed off, the island's assembly made known its gratitude to Queen Victoria for this unprecedented voluntary withdrawal by a great power from an overseas possession.

Peace settled on the island in its early years as a province of Greece. Aristocratic tourists converged here, including Empress Elisabeth of Austria, who liked it so much that she commissioned the grandiose Achilleion Palace.

Palace of St Michael and St George

Although royalist Greece was officially neutral during the first three years of World War I, Venezelist-republican Corfu effectively served as an Allied military and naval base. In early 1916 Corfu gave refuge to the exiled government of Serbia and its troops as they fled defeat at the hands of the Bulgarians and Austrians. Thousands died from wounds and disease, buried both on Vídos islet and at sea adjacent, but many more recovered at camps across the island, beginning a long-standing mutual love affair between Serbia and Corfu. By April 1916, 130,000 of them were well enough to be sent, without losses, on French and British ships to fight on the Salonika front.

On 31 August 1923 Mussolini ordered his fleet to bombard the island in reprisal for the murder of four high-ranking Italian officers on the Albanian-Greek border. Italian forces occupied Corfu for most of September until League of Nations mediations saw their withdrawal in exchange for a Greek apology and payment of reparations. The Italians returned as occupiers during World War II, from spring 1941 until Italy capitulated in September 1943.

When the Germans tried to succeed their defeated allies, the Italian troops (who had now switched sides) resisted on Corfu and throughout the Ionian islands. In the ensuing battles and bombardments, nearly a quarter of Kérkyra Town was destroyed, including the parliament house, academy and municipal theatre. After a year of occupation, during which the thriving Jewish community was deported to its death, German forces evacuated Corfu in October 1944. The British moved in, and peace reigned once more.

Corfu was largely unaffected by the Greek civil war between communist and royalist armies that raged on the mainland between 1947 and 1949, though in light of its rebellious republican past it was garrisoned by a special gendarmerie. Since then, tourism, real estate sales and agriculture – the three economic mainstays of the island – have brought unprecedented prosperity to much of Corfu, though more recently it has been markedly affected by the post-2008 global economic downturn and the 2010–onwards Greek debt crisis.

Tourism helps to boost Corfu's economy

Historical Landmarks

734BC Corinthians found colony of Korkyra.

665BC Korkyra defeats Corinth and gains independence.

229BC–AD336 Romans control Corfu, their first colony in the Adriatic.

336 Corfu becomes part of Byzantine Empire.

562 Ostrogoths devastate ancient Korkyra and its monuments.

933 Byzantine Corfiots establish new capital and build first fortress.

1185 Normans seize Corfu after several attempts.

1204 Fall of Constantinople to Fourth Crusade; Venice acquires Corfu.

1214–59 Despotate of Epirus controls Corfu.

1259–1386 Kings of Sicily, mostly of the Angevin dynasty, rule Corfu.

1386 Venetian occupation establishes Corfu as a key commercial port and naval base.

1537 Kérkyra Town withstands first Turkish siege; countryside sacked.

1572–1645 Venice erects great city walls and fortresses at Kérkyra.

1716 Corfiots, Venetians and allies repel Ottoman siege of Corfu.

1797 Napoleon defeats Venice, which cedes Ionian Islands to France.

1799–1807 Russians and Turks seize Corfu; 'Septinsular Republic' set up by Russia.

1807–14 Ionian Islands again taken by French.

1814–63 Corfu becomes a British protectorate.

1828 Mainland Greece wins independence from Turkey.

1864 Britain dissolves protectorate, cedes Ionian Islands to Greece.

1916 Corfu gives refuge to exiled Serbian government.

1941 Corfu surrenders to Italy.

1943 Kérkyra Town badly damaged by German bombardment. Nazis occupy Corfu.

1944 Corfu liberated by the Allies.

1994 The island hosts the European Union Summit.

2002 Greece adopts the euro.

2004 Greece wins Euro 2004 and hosts Olympic Games in Athens.

2010–11 Greek debt burden becomes unmanageable; Greece goes under IMF/EU supervision.

WHERE TO GO

Although Kérkyra Town (Corfu Town) is the heart and soul of the island, like most capitals it is neither typical nor representative. Unless you are travelling independently or just visiting Corfu briefly, it is unlikely that you will be staying overnight in Kérkyra Town.

The vast majority of Corfu's visitors are on package tours and invariably stay on the coast at a broad range of accommodation – from cheap-and-cheerful hotels to luxury villas. Nonetheless, Kérkyra Town acts as a magnet for shoppers, culture vultures, or the merely curious, and it rarely disappoints. Located about halfway down the east coast, it is within striking distance of any spot on the island and thus makes a useful reference point for us to begin our island tour.

We shall divide this tour as follows:

The South. The long, narrow southern portion of the island is often described (usually by people who haven't been to Corfu) as nothing more than a party zone. This is certainly true of its extremity (Kávos) but is not the case when applied to the whole area. The Achilleion Palace is Corfu's most-visited cultural attraction, while the long laid-back beaches of Ágios Geórgios Argyrádon and peaceful fishing villages such as Boúkari provide a sharp contrast to the busy resorts of Benítses, Moraïtika and Mesongí.

North of Kérkyra Town. Immediately north of the capital is the most developed part of the island. Its resorts are mostly hidden from the main road, occupying the large bays and inlets on this stretch of coastline.

The Northeast. Look at any website or brochure for expensive Corfu villas and you will find most are in the small area

Enjoying Barbáti beach, in the Northeast

between Barbáti and Kassiópi. The Durrells made Kalámi the most famous resort on this stretch, but there are many similar ones nestling in the exquisite tiny coves that make this area 'connoisseur's Corfu'. A short distance inland looms Mt Pandokrátor.

The North and Northwest. While the north coast is well developed and dominated by the resorts of Sidári and Róda, the northwest remains something of a mystery to many visitors. The resorts of Ágios Geórgios Págon and Ágios Stéfanos Gýrou are very different from their namesakes south and east, respectively. The jewel of the northwest is Paleokastrítsa, boasting one of the most beautiful bays in all of Europe and retaining some charm despite its huge popularity.

The West. Between Érmones and Ágios Górdis, the west coast has superb sandy beaches. Despite often tricky road access, they are no secret any longer, and mostly well-developed.

KÉRKYRA TOWN

Kérkyra Town ❶ (Corfu Town) is a beguiling place, with a relaxed, old-world elegance that rivals other Mediterranean cities many times its size. Its predominantly Venetian architecture is harmoniously flavoured with French and English Georgian building styles, reflecting the influence of several centuries of foreign occupation. A cosmopolitan nature prevails, especially at night, when Corfiots and visitors stroll along the Listón and rendezvous at the many cafés and restaurants. In early August the atmosphere is very Italian.

In Corfu Town

Around the Spianáda (Esplanade)

The focal point of Kérkyra Town is the **Spianáda** (Esplanade) **Ⓐ**. Families promenade, marching bands parade and festive occasions are frequently celebrated on this broad green expanse separating the Old Fort from the rest of town. Buildings formerly here were razed in Venetian times to give a clear field of fire against enemy assault, and it was also used for fairs and jousting tournaments. The French later planted the trees and flower gardens.

Arriving in the Capital

If you are driving into Kérkyra Town, it's best to park just south of the old town, in the vicinity of the Archaeological Museum, especially along Dimokratías Avenue, where street parking is free. Parking at the old harbour, or along the Spianáda, tempting as that might seem, is heavily controlled and expensive. Driving in Kérkyra Town is less stressful than its myriad streets would suggest, thanks to an efficient one-way system.

Public buses set down either at San Rocco Square (blue urban buses) or near the New Fort (green long-distance buses). San Rocco Square (Sarókko in Greek) can be intimidatingly busy at most times of the day. Although it is only a stone's throw away from the tourist centre of Corfu, this is a very 'Greek' part of town, with most shops and businesses – especially along Georgíou Theotóki leading up to the Puorta Reale entrance to the old town – catering to locals. Visitors who arrive by coach excursion disembark close to the Old Fort and the grassy gardens of the Spianáda. Those arriving by ferry at the new harbour will find it a good 1,500-metre (just under 1 mile) walk into town (occasional buses); for airport details see page 115.

Our description of the town inevitably involves some backtracking and close reading of the back-flap map. Kérkyra Town might be a relatively small place, but it is impossible to do justice in a single day. You should certainly aim to come here on Tuesday, Thursday or Friday, when shops open in the evening.

On the southern half of the Spianáda is the plain **Ionian Monument**, which celebrates the island's union with Greece in 1864. It is surrounded by marble reliefs displaying the symbols of the seven Ionian Islands, known as the Eptánisa in Greek. Nearby is the Victorian bandstand (where Sunday concerts are held in summer) and the Maitland Rotunda, dedicated to the first British high commissioner. At the far end is the statue of Greece's first president (1827–31) and Corfu's greatest son, Ioannis Kapodistrias.

The Esplanade's most famous landmark is the now somewhat abbreviated cricket pitch dominating its northern half. Corfu adopted this sport during British rule, and enthusiastic local teams keep the tradition alive with matches during the season.

That's Cricket

Kérkyra Town cricket pitch is one of the most unusual sportsgrounds in the world. Kim Hughes, the Australian captain during the early 1980s, once hit a mighty six right over the gardens and into the moat of the Old Fort here.

The mixed cultural heritage of the island can be heard in the cricketing language. *'Play'* is the Corfiot name for cricket. But, perhaps because of the long association with the Venetians, more than one term used during play has been lifted from Italian. So when a 'long hop' becomes *primo salto* and cricket stumps are *xýla* ('woods' in Greek), the English might feel at a loss in their own game. Still, when the former England captain David Gower was asked where he had enjoyed playing the most, his immediate reply was: 'It has to be Corfu'.

Today the cricket pitch in Kérkyra Town is mainly used by the island's under-18 and under-14 youth teams, since the size of the pitch was reduced to make room for a car park. Adult matches take place in the newer cricket ground at Gouvia Marina.

Across the north side of the Spianáda stands the imposing **Palace of St Michael and St George**  erected between 1819 and 1824 by Maltese masons as the residence for the British high commissioners, with a neoclassical façade of 32 Doric columns linking triumphal arches. It also housed the Ionian senate. When the British left, Greek royalty used it as a summer residence. The bronze toga-

Palace of St Michael and St George

clad figure which stands above a lily pond in front of the palace is Sir Frederick Adam, Britain's second high commissioner. The pool and its waterspouts are there to remind people that Adam was the first to ensure Kérkyra Town a reliable water supply, with an aqueduct system still in use today.

The palace's state rooms now house the **Museum of Asian Art** (spring/autumn Tue–Sun 8.30am–3pm, summer until 7.30pm; charge). Its collection of nearly 11,000 Asian artefacts is one of the most comprehensive of its kind in the world. Pieces in the original east wing include funerary statuary and bowls, pottery and blue-and-white porcelain from various Chinese dynasties. The newer, west wing features a superb miscellany donated in 1974: Hindu and Jain deities, Gandhara relief work, Buddhist devotional art from every south Asian nation. There are also Japanese folding screens and painted hanging scrolls, as well as woodblock prints by such masters as Hokusai and Utamaro.

Around the back of the palace (on the Old Fort side), facing lovely seaview gardens, is the lesser-known **Municipal Art Gallery** (daily summer 9am–5pm, winter 9am–4pm;

The elegant Listón façade

charge), a modest, eight-room collection comprising mostly 19th- and 20th-century works by Corfiot artists. Look for the *Assassination of Kapodistrias* in Room 2, portraying the murder of the island's most famous native son, as well as George Samartzis' charming, French-inspired *Night in Corfu* in Room 5, which shows that even in 1913 the Listón was the place to be. Room 3 contains several fine 16th-century icons, two by the refugee Cretan master Mihaïl Damaskinos. After browsing the pictures, enjoy a coffee and cake in the delightful setting of the adjacent Art Gallery Café.

On the opposite side of the palace, just across the street, stands a pretty yellow building with an arcaded façade, and an outside staircase. This is home to the **Anagnostikí Etería Kérkyras** (Corfu Reading Society), the oldest cultural institution in modern Greece, founded in 1836, housing a vast archive of photographs, books, manuscripts and other documents. However, casual visitors are regarded with suspicion.

The elegant arcades of the **Listón**  border the west side of the Spianáda. Inspired by the Rue de Rivoli in Paris, it was erected by the French in 1807. Its name comes from the 'list' of noble families who (despite notional Napoleonic liberation) were the only ones initially permitted to walk here. These days everyone gathers at the many cafés and bars under the arches or beneath the trees along the green. During the evening pedestrianised Eleftherías out front is transformed into a bustling promenade of Corfiots and visitors alike, from dapper elderly men to smartly dressed families.

Stroll down the length of **Kapodistríou Street**, which runs from behind the Listón to the southern end of the green. It is lined with handsome townhouses, most of which were built by the Venetian-era aristocracy, and several picturesque perpendicular streets lead off into town. Moustoxýdou Street, for example, used to be an important thoroughfare and was also the setting for jousting displays during Carnival, with the judges seated on the balcony above the ornate portico of the Ricchi mansion. At the very end of Kapodistríou, on Ioníou Akadimías, looms the pink façade of the former Ionian Academy, founded in 1824 by Lord Guilford as the first modern Greek university. Like much of the surrounding area, it has been completely rebuilt after suffering destruction in the heavy bombing of 1943, and today appropriately is used by the University of the Ionian.

Shopping in Corfu Town

Dousmáni Street cuts across the Esplanade to the Old Fort. Here you will find a string of colourful 19th-century horse-cabs (*carrozzi*), which will take you on a ride around Kérkyra Town. Be sure to agree on the fare before you set out.

The Paleó Froúrio (Old Fort)

Kérkyra Town grew up on the eastern peninsula around the **Paleó Froúrio**  (Old Fort; summer Mon–Fri 8.30am–7pm (to 3pm winter), Sat–Sun 8.30am–3pm; charge), first established by the Byzantines during the 6th century after the Ostrogoth raids. The two peaks of the promontory on which it stands were the source of the name Corfu, a corruption of *koryfí* (summit in Greek).

A statue of Count Johann Matthias von der Schulenburg, the German mercenary who led the Corfiot defence against the Turkish attack of 1716, stands outside the fortress's west gate, one of the many fortifications added by the Venetians to the older Byzantine citadel on the eastern peak. Its defensive moat, the Contrafossa, is lined with small fishing boats and utility sheds, making for a very picturesque and peaceful scene. In turbulent times in the past, the bridge beyond the gate could be raised, cutting off land access to the fort.

The Old Fort on its promontory

The Venetian administration was based here; subsequently the British built barracks and a military hospital. The fort was then used by the Greek army until 1979. Restoration since then has included transforming the gatehouse into an excellent, small Byzantine museum (admission included in the fort ticket) containing bird mosaics from the Iovianós Basilica at Paleópolis, plus late Byzantine frescoes from a church in Káto Korakiána.

Combined ticket

You can save a considerable amount on site admissions by buying a combined ticket for €10. This allows entry to the Archaeological Museum, the Museum of Asian Art, the Byzantine Museum and the Old Fort, over a period of a few days.

Once inside the fort complex, a path to the right leads to the neoclassical garrison church of **Ágios Geórgios**, built by the British in 1840 as an Anglican chapel and restored after damage during World War II. Now converted to a Greek Orthodox church, it has a fine stone iconostasis and icons but, thanks partly to its origins, is plain and box-like inside; interior columns disappeared during the restoration.

Come back toward the entrance, where a stone path leads past a Venetian clocktower up to the lighthouse on the higher peak. The steep climb is well worth it for the spectacular panorama of Kérkyra Town, the harbour, the mainland coast and Mt Pandokrátor to the north.

From the Listón to the Néo Froúrio

From the northern end of the Listón, walk along Kapodistríou Street, past the Corfu Reading Society, and enter Arseníou Street. Look back to your right for a fine view of the Old Fort and its marina. Immediately below you is the small promontory of **Faliráki ❺**, with a clutch of cafés, snack bars and a swimming lido.

The densely wooded islet just offshore is **Vídos Island**, today a nature reserve but once a base for the Ottoman attacks of 1537 and 1716. More famously, the island served as a quarantine station for the most hopeless cases of the 150,000-strong Serbian army which retreated to Corfu in early 1916. About

1,200 casualties were buried on the island itself (they are now comemmorated by a mausoleum), but the burial capacity of rocky Vídos was soon exceeded, and almost 10,000 more were buried at sea adjacent, an episode immortalised in the poem by Serb Milutin Bojić, *Plava Grobica* (Blue Grave – also with a memorial plaque on Vídos). Today, boats regularly shuttle between the island and the Old Port.

A short way along Arseníou Street, a flight of steps leads to the excellent **Mousío Andivouniótissas** (Byzantine Museum) **F**, housed in the eponymous 15th-century basilica (Tue–Sun 8.30am–3pm; charge). The single-aisle, timber-roofed church is one of the oldest and richest on the island, with an *exonarthex* (vestibule) surrounding it on three sides. This is used today to exhibit an impressive array of icons from the 15th to 19th centuries, many of the so-called 'Cretan School'; after the fall of Crete to

The Byzantine Museum occupies a 15th-century basilica

the Ottomans, many highly skilled artists came as refugees to Venetian-held Corfu.

Around the corner, the imposing profile of the **Néo Froúrio** (New Fort)  (daily 8.30am–3pm, until 7pm summer; charge) heaves into view beyond the Old Port. The New Fort (also known as the Fort of San Marco) was built by the Venetians between 1572 and 1645, shortly after the first major Ottoman siege. You can see the Venetian emblem – the winged lion of St Mark – in stone relief above the massive gates. The French, and later the British, elaborated the fortifications. The town's fruit and vegetable market is now held in the dry moat on the western side. A series of secret tunnels is said to connect the new and old fortresses (and even Vídos). Occasionally, temporary exhibitions or concerts are held inside the walls, but the finest sight is the superb view of Kérkyra Town and the mainland coast.

The New Fort

The Commercial Centre

The town centre essentially lies between the New Fort and the Esplanade, a warren of narrow, pedestrianised, marble-paved lanes arranged in discrete, historic districts. The main commercial artery, linking the Listón and the old harbour in Spiliá district, is **Nikifórou Theotóki** – just one of several thoroughfares named after members of this long-established, illustrious Corfiot family. To the south, in Pórta Remoúnda district, and north, in the Kofinéta neighbourhood, numerous parallel streets intersect Kapodistríou.

The belltower of Ágios Spyrídon

The main square along Nikifórou Theotóki is officially **Platía Iróön Kypriakón Agonistón** (Square of the Cypriot Fighters), with a statue of Corfiot politician Georgios Theotoki (1843–1916) in the middle; however, because the west side of the plaza is bounded by the 1846-vintage building which once housed the island's oldest bank, the Ioniki (Ionian), everybody calls it **Platía Ionikí**. Four galleries on the upper storey above the present-day Alpha Bank here are home to the **Banknote Museum Ⓗ** (summer Mon–Sat 9am–1pm; free), featuring an extensive display of every Greek drachma (the pre-2002 currency) denomination issued as well as Ionian Bank shares and documents. More interesting than it sounds, this impressive collection illustrates all the stages in designing, printing and releasing notes for circulation.

Across from the bank stands the **Faneroméni** church, also called **Panagía ton Xénon** (Our Lady of the Foreigners) because it was used by refugees from the mainland during the Ottoman occupation. Erected in 1689, it is lavishly decorated with gilded wood, a beautifully painted ceiling and icons by Cretan painters. Opposite is a simpler church, **Ágios Ioánnis o Pródromos** (St John the Baptist). Built in 1520, it was formerly Corfu's cathedral and also contains important Cretanschool icons.

The red-domed belltower of the church of **Ágios Spyrídon ①**, the tallest on the island, rises north of the square, at the top of the broad stairway known as the Plakáda t'Agíou. It was founded in 1590 to house the mummified body of Corfu's beloved patron saint, who lies in an ornate silver coffin in a shrine to the right of the altar. On certain days the casket is opened, and on special feast days the saint is paraded upright through the town. His shrunken face can be seen through a glass panel, and his slippered feet are exposed for the faithful to kiss. With all the opulent Venetian oil lamps swinging above the casket (plus the chandeliers and the candelabra), this modest, dimly lit church is said to have the greatest amount of silver of any Greek church outside the island of Tínos. Frescoes on the ceiling depict the saint's miracles.

Leave the church by the door giving onto Agíou Spyrídonos Street, turning left to meet Filarmonikís Street. Here you can

St Spyridon

Corfiots pray to him, swear by him, name their sons after him and honour him with a remarkable passion. He is the island's beloved patron saint, yet he wasn't even born on Corfu. Spyridon was a village shepherd on the distant island of Cyprus. He became a monk, then a bishop, and was noted for his devoutness and ability to effect minor miracles. After his death in AD348, a sweet odour wafted from his grave; his body was exhumed and found to be perfectly preserved. The saint's remains were taken to Constantinople but were smuggled out (with those of St Theodora Augusta) before the Turkish occupation in 1453. Unceremoniously wrapped in a sack of straw strapped to a mule, the remains arrived in Corfu in 1456. In time, Spyridon became the object of enthusiastic veneration.

To honour his miracles, his casket is paraded through Kérkyra Town in colourful processions on Orthodox Palm Sunday, Easter Saturday, 11 August, and the first Sunday in November. St Spyridon has reputedly saved the island four times: twice from the plague, once from famine, and once (in 1716) from the Turks. Small wonder that numerous Corfiot men are named Spyros.

The marble-clad Town Hall

turn right to explore the Campiello district (see page 42). Or you can turn left to reach M. Theotóki Street to see more of the shopping district. (If you have time do both, see the Old Town first and then retrace your steps.)

Follow M. Theotóki Street south, past the lovely, compact **Platía Vrahlióti** with a well in the centre, until emerging onto tiered **Platía Dimarhíou ❶** (Town Hall Square), officially Platía Mihaïl Theotóki. At the bottom end sits the **Dimarhío** (**Town Hall**), one of Corfu's most decorative buildings. Built by the Venetians in 1665 out of white marble from the eastern slopes of Mt Pandokrátor, its original single-storey loggia served as a meeting place for the nobility. It was converted into the San Giacomo Theatre in 1720, and later a second storey was added. It became the Town Hall in 1903 when the municipal theatre (destroyed in 1943) was constructed. The façade is adorned with carved masks and medallions. On the eastern wall there is a bust of

Francesco Morosini, the Venetian commander who defeated the Ottomans at Athens in 1687.

The tiers of the plaza are crowded with the tables of a popular café and expensive, touristy restaurants; in off hours local boys find the layout irresistible for skateboarding. The imposing building diagonally opposite the Dimarhío is the **Catholic Cathedral of Ágii Iákovos ke Hristóforos** (SS James and Christopher), dating from 1632. It is frequently open for use by Corfu's large Catholic community, about 3,000 strong and entirely descended from 19th-century Maltese stonemasons brought here by the British.

From Platía Dimarhíou, continue south into the lanes of Pórta Remoúnda, where the main sight, at Moustoxýdou 19, is the **Serbian Museum** Ⓚ (Mon–Sat 9am–2pm; free), which with military paraphernalia, documents and photographs meticulously documents the experiences of the Serbian army and government-in-exile here during World War I, when over 100,000 soldiers rested at scattered campsites between Pyrgí and Moraïtika from January 1916 onwards. Besides Greece, the only one of their notional allies who provided supplies or medical assistance to the defeated army in an official capacity was France – though a period poster, issued by a US-based relief committee, makes interesting reading ('Save Serbia, Our Ally') in light of the American 1990s demonisation of the country. The refugees got on famously with their hosts – there were no reports of looting or other improper behaviour – and a number of marriages with local girls resulted, as about 10,000 Serbs stayed on Corfu until 1918.

In the heart of the Campiello

The Old Town

The **Old Town** is the fascinating maze of narrow streets, steep stairways and arched alleys squeezed into the northern half of Kérkyra Town, between the Spianáda and the Old Port. It has been described as Greece's largest 'living medieval town'. As you wander along the marble-paved streets, you might feel that this traffic-free quarter of tottering multi-storey buildings is like a miniature Venice – minus the canals, of course; the northern-most part has even retained its Venetian name, **Campiello Ⓛ**. There are many ways of entering the Campiello, and it is an excellent place to simply wander at will.

In Venetian times, the area between the old and new forts was surrounded by city walls (demolished during the 19th century). As Corfiots weren't permitted to live outside the fortifications, the only direction in which they could expand their dwellings was upwards, producing the district's unusually high architecture. And, just as in the less-touristy parts of Venice, much of the district's appeal is in its residential atmosphere, with laundry strung across alleyways, old women sitting on stools weaving or keeping an eye on babies, and cats snoozing in tiny sun-splashed squares. The only 'sight' is the charming 17th-century **Venetian Well** on the Campiello's Platía Kremastí (officially Líla Desýlla), where a notable restaurant sets out its tables.

From just below Platía Kremastí, Agías Theodóras Street leads to Corfu's **Orthodox Cathedral Ⓜ**, built in 1577 and dedicated to St Theodora Augusta, the island's second-most-revered saint (after Spyridon). Her headless body, which was spirited out of Constantinople (along with Spyridon's), lies in a silver reliquary to the right of the altar screen. Broad flights of steps lead down to the harbour, and Corfiots often momentarily pause here to light a candle before or after embarking on a sea journey.

From just below the cathedral, traverse restaurant-and-café-rich Spiliá district along Prosaléndou, then Solomoú, streets,

The massive Gorgon pediment in the Archaeological Museum

watching for signs indicating Corfu's sole surviving synagogue in the old Evraïkí (Jewish) quarter. The **Scuola Greca** **N** (May–Sept Mon–Fri 8am–7pm; donation) at Velisaríou 4 has been lovingly restored, and the upstairs prayer hall has a memorial plaque to the 1,900 local Jews deported to Auschwitz in June 1944. The local community of about 60 is now too small to support a rabbi; one comes from Israel for the major holidays.

Archaeological Treasures

From either the Scuola Greca or the Serbian Museum, it's a short, pleasant walk south – along the coastal avenue in the latter case – to the island's **Archaeological Museum** **O** (5 Vraïla Street; Tue–Sun 8.30am–3pm; charge).

This airy, modern building houses superb artefacts from all periods of ancient Korkyra. The star attraction, the **Gorgon pediment** (*c.*585BC) comes from the Temple of Artemis

The verdant tranquillity of the British Cemetery

and is so named for its central sculpted Medusa (the most
infamous of the three snake-haired gorgons), shown here with
wings at her shoulders, winged sandals, and serpents at her
waist. She is flanked by her offspring, born from her dying
blood: Pegasus, the winged horse, and the hero Khrysaor.
Beside her stand two alert lion-panthers waiting to obey the
commands of this monster who, according to myth, turned
anyone who met her gaze to stone. The pediment was discovered in 1912 at Paleópolis and is Greece's oldest existing
monumental sculpture. What makes it particularly fearsome
are the bulging eyes and the sheer scale: she stands some 3m
(10ft) tall.

Not so colossal – but almost as important archaeologically
– is the Archaic Lion of Menekrates in an adjoining room.
This late 7th-century BC sculpture, in near-perfect condition,
was found in 1843 and is thought to have graced the grave of
a warrior during Korkyra's struggle for independence from

Corinth. It is considered one of the most beautiful ancient animal sculptures.

Among the museum's other treasures, unjustly eclipsed by the Gorgon pediment, is a small pediment from 500BC, showing the god Dionysos and a youth reclining at a symposium, holding a *rhyton* (pouring vessel) and a *kylix* (drinking cup) respectively. Their banqueting couch is supported by two lions. Nearby stand a dozen small statues of the goddess Artemis in her avatar as mistress of beasts; they are thought to have been produced as votive offerings for local worshippers.

Some three blocks southwest of the museum stands the **tomb of Menekrates**, on Maraslí, a circular structure with a conical roof honouring a mercenary who fought for Korkyra. It dates from about 600BC. Continue inland along this street, then west onto Kolokotróni, to the serenely beautiful **British Cemetery ℗**. Among the tall cypress trees and meticulously kept flowers and shrubbery (beautiful wild flowers, even orchids, also grow here) lie civilian graves dating from 1814 to recent years. There are graves of British servicemen from the two World Wars as well. The circular wall south of the cemetery encloses the local **jail** (*fylakí*). Built by the British, it was once the most modern penal institute in Europe, with individual cells for inmates. It is still in use today, though ironically it now has one of the worst reputations in Greece.

Southern Suburbs

To explore this part of Corfu you will need transport, or be willing to hop on and off blue city buses marked '2 KANONI'. Head south along the coastal road for about 2km (a mile or so) and turn inland (right) to the Byzantine **Church of Ágii Iáson ke Sosípatros ℚ** (daily 8.30am–2pm), one of only two Byzantine churches surviving intact on the island. It is dedicated to saints Jason and Sosipater, the evangelists credited

Kardáki Spring

Near the roundabout at Análipsi, a steep path leads down to Kardáki Spring. The water that flows from the mouth of a stone lion – cool in the summer and warm in the winter – is reputed never to dry up. Legend has it that anyone who drinks from the spring is destined to return to Corfu.

with bringing Christianity to Corfu in the 2nd century. The present church dates back to about 1000, and conforms to a type then popular on the Greek mainland – a domed, cross-in-square ground plan with a narthex and triple apse. The black marble columns separating the narthex from the main church, and huge poros blocks in the walls, come from ancient buildings. Few frescoes have survived, but there are fine icons in the Baroque chancel.

Further along the road to Kanóni stands the entrance to the villa and gardens of **Mon Repos ®**. Built in 1820 by High Commissioner Frederick Adam as a summer residence, it later became the property of the Greek royal family. Prince Philip, the Duke of Edinburgh, was born here in 1921. Mon Repos was subsequently the subject of an ownership dispute between ex-king Constantine and the government, only resolved in 1996. Since then the villa has been restored and now contains the Museum of Paleópolis (summer Mon–Fri 8am–7pm, Sat–Sun and daily winter 8am–3pm; charge). While the contents are not generally world-beating, the displays are well-laid out and labelled, with interesting temporary exhibits. There are period furnishings from Adams' time, a useful interactive model of the ancient town and environs, photos of archaeological digs, and a wealth of thematically arranged finds from the grounds of the estate, especially the shrine at Kardáki. Paths outside wind along the wooded promontory, past a derelict chapel, to a scenic viewpoint; from here it's another 15 minutes' walk to the remains of a small Doric temple dating from 500BC.

Ancient Korkyra

Opposite the Mon Repos gate lie the commanding ruins of the originally 5th-century **basilica of Iovianós** 🟢 (Agía Kérkyra; open irregularly), oldest church on the island, constructed from remnants of nearby pagan temples. Once five-aisled, it was ruined by invaders, rebuilt to a smaller scale during ensuing centuries, then destroyed again in World War II before being partially restored in 2000.

The original Corinthian-founded city of Korkyra sprawled over much of the area between Mon Repos and Kanóni, now called **Paleópolis**. A narrow road behind the Roman baths (open) opposite the basilica leads to the hamlet of Análipsi, thought to be the location of the ancient acropolis, unsurprisingly with excellent views over Mon Repos.

Along the road toward Kanóni, you'll see a side road marked 'Stratía'. Here are the ruins of the **Temple of Artemis**, source

The monastery of Panagía Vlahernón off the Kanóni Peninsula

of the Gorgon Pediment. Next door is the well-kept monastery of **Agíon Theodóron**. At the end of this road stands the only surviving section of the ancient city wall, a 5th-century BC tower which in Byzantine times became the church of **Panagía Neratzíha**.

Kanóni

Generations of earlier visitors knew **Kanóni ❷** as a tranquil green peninsula, a pleasant walk or carriage ride south of the capital. Popular with Corfiots, it also used to attract large groups of British residents, who came to admire the most famous view on the island: the two islets resting peacefully in the Halikopoúlou lagoon.

Times have changed, as modern hotels and blocks of flats have disfigured the landscape. The motivation for building here is unclear, as most views are of the shallow, muddy lagoon and the adjacent international airport runway, complete with thunderous sound effects. In fact, it might be said that Kanóni has come full circle: its name derives from the gun battery that the French installed on the hillside here in 1798. Nevertheless, the delightful picture-postcard **view** of the islets and the coastal scenery beyond them remains intact, attracting an endless stream of tour buses to Kanóni.

The islet in the foreground – linked to the mainland by a causeway – is not Mouse Island but **Vlahérna**, which is home to a pretty, white, post-Byzantine convent (Panagía Vlahernón; usually shut). **Mouse Island** (or Pondikonísi) lies a three-minute boat trip away, though in reality it is of little interest and hardly worth the journey. Mouse Island is the main contender for the site of the mythical Odyssean ship turned to stone *(see page 14)*.

A pair of café-restaurants on the hillside provide a relaxing terrace from which to enjoy the magnificent view. A pedestrian causeway below leads across the lagoon to Pérama.

Described by the British writer Lawrence Durrell as 'a monstrous building' and by the American Henry Miller as 'the worst piece of gimcrackery I have ever laid eyes on', the **Achilleion (Ahíllio) Palace** ❸ (daily April–Oct 8am–7pm, Nov–March 8.45am–3.30pm; charge) is one of the most popular sights on the island, and usually teeming with tour groups. Used as a location in the James Bond film *For Your Eyes Only*, the palace is situated some 10km (6 miles) south of Kérkyra Town.

Corfu's most popular tourist sight: the Achilleion Palace

A romantic past as an imperial hideaway forms a large part of the palace's attraction. The beautiful Empress Elisabeth of Austria (nicknamed Sisi) fell in love with this site on a visit to the island during the 1860s. In 1889 – desperately unhappy in her marriage, stifled by the pomp of Vienna and stricken by the suicide of her only son – she bought this land and commissioned the building of a palace that would be worthy of her idol, the Greek hero Achilles. The result, built in extreme neoclassical style, was immediately criticised as being tasteless and ostentatious.

The empress nonetheless spent as much time as she possibly could at the Achilleion, in utmost seclusion in the spring and autumn of each year. But poor Sisi had only seven years to enjoy her palace. Her tragic life came to a premature end in 1898 when, during a visit to Geneva, she was mortally stabbed by an Italian anarchist.

In 1908 Kaiser Wilhelm II of Germany acquired the palace from Sisi's daughter, inviting dignitaries from all over Europe to attend parties and concerts here. Because most arrived by boat, he built a bridge at the seashore that crossed the coastal road to paths leading directly to his palace. Only the ruins of the bridge, ironically destroyed by the German army in 1943, remain today. The Kaiser also installed an awesome 4.5-ton bronze *Victorious Achilles*, which looms some 11.5m (38ft) high at the far end of the formal gardens.

Kaiser Wilhelm's mighty Achilles

ΑΧΙΛΛΕΥΣ

The Achilleion was used as a military hospital during World War I by the Serbs and the French (whose casualties lie in a cemetery just downhill). In 1919 it became the property of the Greek government, as war reparations, and from 1962 to 1983 its opulent upper floors were converted into a casino. In the 1990s, after renovation and the removal of its casino, the palace was opened to the public, though only half a dozen ground-floor rooms can be visited.

The Achilleion is adorned throughout by pseudo-Classical statues, with Greek gods, goddesses and heroes filling every corner. Those surrounding the Peristyle of the Muses, behind the palace, are copies of the ones in Rome's Villa Borghese gardens. Do make sure to peer through the window here to see the giant painting *The Triumph of Achilles* by Franz Matz. (It is on the first floor

Statue highlight

Among all the statues scattered about the grounds, only one is considered by experts to have any artistic merit: the dramatic *Dying Achilles*, by German sculptor Ernst Herter.

of the palace, which is closed to the public.) Our hero is shown in brutal, vengeful form dragging the body of Hector behind his chariot as a reprisal for the killing of Achilles' friend Patroklos.

Inside, the ground-floor rooms house a small chapel and the original furnishings and memorabilia of the empress and the Kaiser. One unusual attraction is the adjustable saddle on which Wilhelm used to sit while writing at his desk.

The extensive grounds are perhaps the true highlight of the Achilleion. The manicured formal gardens are a real pleasure, with magnificent sweeping views over the island.

THE SOUTH

Benítses ❹, some 12km (7.5 miles) south of the capital, used to be the island's nonstop party town, but no longer. It now attracts a much quieter clientele. The town is also revamping its image with the opening of a smart new marina opposite the main square; it is already semi-operational, but awaits completion with Russian funding.

Arriving from the north, the first thing you will see in Benítses is the **Corfu Shell Museum** (Mar–May and Oct daily 10am–6pm, June–Sept 9am–8pm; www.corfushell museum.com; charge). This impressive exhibition of seashells, corals, fossils, starfish and sponges was collected throughout the world by an Australian-Corfiot. The many specimens on display range from huge clamshells to tiny delicate cowries, fearsome shark's jaws, spiny crustacean skeletons and stuffed pufferfish.

Benítses has been settled since at least Roman times; behind the harbour square stand the meagre remains of what was once a Roman bathhouse. This old village centre, near the port, has a very Greek atmosphere, with pretty cottages that retain the character of the original fishing settlement. The lush valley at the western edge of town is crisscrossed with footpaths in an unexpected wilderness.

Moraïtika and Mesongí

The busy coastal road continues south as far as the contiguous resorts of Moraïtika and Mesongí, 20km (12.5 miles) from Kérkyra Town. They lie at the mouth of – and are divided by – the Mesongí river (rowboat ferries cross it). This is an attractive spot, with fishing and pleasure boats

The Venerable Olive

Almost everyone on Corfu owns a few olive trees. In Venetian times, peasants were paid a bonus for every 100 trees planted, and by the 17th century a family's wealth was determined by the number of trees it owned. Today there are said to be 3.5 million of them on the island.

According to legend, St Spyridon appeared in an olive grove and proclaimed that cutting or beating the trees was cruel. As a result, for many years Corfiots neither pruned the branches nor picked the fruit. Instead, they let the olives fall to the ground naturally, where huge nets were spread to catch them. Today, however, pruning – and some combing out of the fruit – is practiced. Trees bear fruit only every other year and might take 12 years to yield a first crop.

moored alongside the riverfront.

Moraïtika ❺ is the busier and livelier of the pair. Its older section is set on a hill just off the main road and marked by a red-and-yellow campanile. There is no tourist development up here, just an attractive taverna or two providing a nice contrast to the seaside resort below. Like

Sea shore taverna at Boúkari

Moraïtika, **Mesongí** ❻ features an increasing amount of development, now spreading back from the long but very narrow beaches. Behind the beach, Mesongí has some of Corfu's oldest olive groves, planted by the Venetians over 500 years ago.

From here the main road south curves inland and reaches a T-junction at Áno Mesongí. The route north takes you inland through the pastoral scenery of the Mesongí river valley before ascending the slopes of Corfu's second-tallest mountain, the 576m (1,889ft) Ágii Déka ('Ten Saints'). From **Ágii Déka village** ❼ there are spectacular views over Benítses and the distant Kanóni Peninsula.

An alternative route to the southern tip of the island involves following the minor road that runs along the coast southeast from Mesongí. Along this peaceful, tree-shaded shore are small seafood tavernas and narrow, pebbly beaches where you can soak up the tranquil bay view. This pretty stretch ends at the small fishing village of **Boúkari**. But if you would like a little more of the same, you can continue along the coast road to Petríti, another quiet spot where fresh fish is a speciality.

Southwest Beaches

Directly opposite here, on Corfu's southwest coast, lies the island's longest sandy beach, divided into various resorts. To reach it from Boúkari, return to the main road where the old monastery at Argyrádes sports a striking Venetian belfry. Head east for 2km (1.2 miles) and at Marathiás village a sign to **Paralía Marathiá** points to the right, down to the beach; the road forks, with the left option skirting a small stream which separates one from the contiguous stretch of beach known as **Agía Varvára** ❽. It's easy enough to ford the stream, but by car the low-key development at Agía Varvára is accessible only by a separate road from Perivóli village. Together they form an attractive broad stretch of soft golden sand, with a few naturists under the cliffs of the Agía Varvára section.

The turning for the much busier resort of **Ágios Geórgios Argyrádon** heads down just west of Argyrádes. Development

Agía Varvára is part of the longest sandy beach on all Corfu

sprawls for about 2km (a mile or so) along the frontage road, but the beach is as good as Agía Varvára or Marathiá, made of the same golden sand. The resort strip ends at bit further west at **Íssos ❾** beach, which borders the lagoon of Korissíon. Drivers are better off returning to the main road, head west and then descending

The Korission Lagoon

This lagoon was artificially created with a channel from the sea by the Venetians as a fish nursery, for which purpose it is still used. Today it is a protected area, off-limits for swimming or boating, but bird-watchers will find plenty to observe here, in spring or autumn.

at the signposted turning. The scenery at Íssos is quite wild, with high dunes providing shelter for nudists, and large wind-carved rock outcrops. This was a setting for a chase scene in the James Bond film *For Your Eyes Only*. Windsurfing conditions are excellent, and a small school operates locally.

On the far side of the channel which feeds the brackish lagoon is **Halikoúnas** beach, perhaps not quite as spectacular as Íssos but also with a kite-surfing school, pockets of naturism, beach bars and a better selection of full-service tavernas at the far end. Road access is via Áno Mesongí, past a memorial to the Serbian Drina Division and the Byzantine **castle of Gardíki ❿** (closed for restoration).

Kávos

Southeast of Marathiás sprawls a fertile landscape dvoted to fruit orchards, market gardens, yet more olive groves and Corfu's principal wine-producing region. **Lefkímmi** is the hub of this working agricultural region, bypassed by a very fast road that goes all the way to the southern tip of the island. **Kávos ⓫** is the end of the road, the last resort – in just about every respect. To Corfiots and foreigners alike, the name is synonymous with young booze-fuelled revellers, clubbing

Pier at Dassiá

and partying. But lately its abundant accommodation and dozen music clubs work to half-capacity at best, even in July and August. That said, the soft sandy beach that extends for 3km (nearly 2 miles) shelves gently and is popular with families earlier in the season. Boat excursions leave from here as well.

About 3km south lies Cape Asprókavos, Corfu's southernmost tip, and the disused **monastery of Panagía Arkoudílas,** overlooking the superb beach of Kánoula.

NORTH OF KÉRKYRA TOWN

The former fishing villages northwest of Kérkyra Town are now home to some of the island's liveliest and most popular resorts. Kondókali and Gouviá lie within a sheltered lagoon about 8km (5 miles) from the capital. They are set back from the busy main highway and linked by a small road, with side tracks leading to sand and pebble beaches and a large marina.

Gouviá ⓬ is the more developed of the two, with a narrow, compacted sand beach dominated by large hotels. One section is even fronted with concrete so that the sea (shallow and still at this point) looks more like a municipal boating pond than the Ionian. The sheltered bay is largely taken up by an extensive yacht marina – appropriately enough, as it was once a Venetian naval base and the skeletal arches of an old Venetian *arsenáli* (boatyard) survive at the end of Gouviá's beach.

Across the pretty bay you can see the little church of **Ypapandí** (Candlemas; Presentation of Christ), which juts out on a stone spit rather like the famous 'Mouse Island' vista. Beyond the confines of the lagoon is **Lazarétto**  island, with a grim history – the Venetians established a leprosarium on it, the World War II occupying powers confined (and shot) members of the Greek resistance here, and after the the Greek civil war it served as a place for executing condemned communists.

The resort of **Dassiá** features dense olive groves between the main road and the sea, but otherwise consists merely of a long string of restaurants, shops and bars along a very busy main road. A long, narrow and often crowded beach is tucked away down side roads, with various watersports on offer. The continual stream of colourful parasails against the blue sky – with olive groves and mountains in the background – is a fine sight.

Watersports at Ýpsos

To escape the hustle and bustle, wander inland on an uphill journey past quiet villas and olive groves to **Káto Korakiána** ⑭. Here, installed in an old, three-storey Venetian villa, is the **National Gallery Annexe of Corfu** (Mon–Wed 10am–2pm and 6–9pm, Thur, Fri, Sun 10am–3pm, Sat 10am–2pm; charge). There are 150 works of prominent Greek painters from all eras since 1830, on permanent loan from the Athens parent collection.

The contiguous resorts of **Ýpsos** and **Pyrgí** flank a wide, beautiful bay about 15km (9.5 miles) north of Kérkyra Town. They have fallen somewhat on hard times, and are trying to re-invent themselves as family havens after many years of patronage by armies of young, largely British singles. The long, narrow beach lining the bay is a mixture of sand and shingle, with excellent water sports facilities.

In times past, Ýpsos Bay was a target for pirates and Ottoman raiders; supposedly the name *Ýpsos* ('heights') was a ruse to dissuade them from mounting an attack. *Pyrgí*, meaning 'tower', probably derives from watchtowers built to warn of imminent raids. The resorts themselves are recent creations, developing around resettlements of villagers from Ágios Márkos whose homes were destroyed by landslides in the 1950s. Ýpsos at least has retained its fishing fleet, tucked away in an attractive little harbour behind the road as you enter from the south.

Icon at Ypsilóu Pandokrátora

The tranquil old village of **Ágios Márkos** 🄯, signposted just outside Pyrgí, is worth a detour for glorious views of the coastline, and two churches. At the top of the village is the 16th-century Church of Christ Pandokrátor, with fresco-covered walls. Some 500m/yds south of the village, 11th-century Ágios Merkoúrios and Profítis Ilías

is Corfu's oldest Byzantine
church, with vivid frescoes
including Saint Marina slay-
ing the devil on the north
wall. This church is usually
locked; the priest, who lives
in Pyrgí by the health clinic,
keeps the key.

Making the ascent

It is also possible to get to the
top of Mt Pandokrátor from
the northeastern part of the
island (see page 65). A good
tour choice is to go up one
side and come down the other.

Mt Pandokrátor

Just beyond the Ágios Márkos turn-off, a road leads to the
top of **Mt Pandokrátor** (914m/2,833ft). Beyond a series of
corkscrew bends you'll be greeted by stupendous views over
Ýpsos Bay. Just below the colourful village of Spartýlas, the
road broadens out into a rolling landscape of fruit trees,
fields and vineyards where some of Corfu's finest wine is produced. Between Strinýlas and Petália, signs indicate the final
approach to Mt Pandokrátor.

This side road is emphatically not to be driven in bad
weather, and parking space at the summit is limited – best
to leave cars below the final zigzag and walk up the last
hundred meters. On a clear day you will be rewarded with
unbeatable views: the entire sickle outline of Corfu and,
over the narrow channel, a glimpse of Albania. To the south,
in the blue Ionian Sea, lie the islands of Paxí and distant
Lefkáda. Sadly, closer up the view now includes the after-
math of an August 2011 forest fire which devastated much
of Mt Pandokrátor.

The summit monastery of **Ypsiloú Pandokrátora** ⑯ (Apr–
Oct 7am–12.30pm and 2.30–8pm; free), which shares space
with an ugly, 86m (280ft) antenna erected by the 1967–74 military junta to beam propaganda into Albania, was constructed
during the 17th century on the site of a 1347 vintage church
that had been built by nearby villagers. Restored in recent

Relaxing on Nisáki's tiny beach

years, it is a dark, peaceful haven with many frescoes and an ornate icon screen, but just one monk.

THE NORTHEAST

The dramatic beauty of northeastern Corfu begins above Ýpsos Bay and ends near Kassiópi, a lovely drive over a winding, narrow but paved road covering some 20km (12.5 miles). The road climbs sharply into the steep green slopes that overawe the coast, offering tantalising glimpses of the sea below. There are several viewing points along this cliffside road, but most of the shore is hidden and often accessible only by narrow, steep tracks that plunge alarmingly. Some beaches can be reached only on foot. The best way to explore is by boat, which can be arranged from most jetties – self-skippering boat-hire is very popular here. It is worth noting that all the beaches from Ýpsos to Kassiópi are pebbly. Nonetheless, swimming is excellent at nearly all the beaches along this coast.

The shift from the mass-market resorts south of Ýpsos Bay to the small and relatively less-developed coves of the north-east peninsula comes at **Barbáti** ⑰. There is no steep track to negotiate here, just a gentle slope leading down to sea level, where olive groves shelter a long, pebbly and popular beach with all the usual water sports. The mountains rise steeply behind the beach, making an attractive backdrop. There is some music from beachside and roadside bars, but the atmosphere of Barbáti is very different from that of its southern neighbours.

The next resort along is **Nisáki** ⓲, reached by a two-bend drive from the main road. The water here is a crystal-clear medley of greens and blues, though there is hardly room to spread your towel on its tiny pebble beach. It is undoubtedly a lovely spot, with tavernas, a cluster of shops and accommodation, but you will have to get here early (or late) to stake a beach claim.

Just a bit further on, **Kamináki** is a strong contender in the sweepstakes for 'Corfu's most terrifying beach descent'. There are two tavernas, a small watersports facility and around 100m (330ft) of attractive white-pebble beach. The next beach along, **Krouzerí**, is dominated by the large Nisáki Beach Hotel. You will have to share the pebbles with hotel guests but the beach is of reasonable size, and there are good water-sports facilities.

A Glimpse of Albania

All along its northeast coast, Corfu looks across at the mainland of Albania. At its nearest point – on the stretch between Kalámi and Ágios Stéfanos – the shore of this now-welcoming, ex-communist land is less than 2 nautical miles away. Day trips are a popular, if somewhat expensive, means of taking a quick look. The boat journey from Kérkyra Town to the Albanian port of Sarandë (Ágii Saránda) takes 40–75 minutes round trip depending on the type of craft used. Outings vary from the basic crossing, guided tour of ancient Butrint and buffet lunch (around €60) to a more elaborate trip including an inland foray to the heritage town of Gjirokastër and Lëkurësi castle near Sarandë (around €95). Agencies in every resort offer these excursions, but you can also book directly through the shipping companies, Petrakis Ionian Cruises, at the New Port (tel: 26610 31649/38690; www.ionian-cruises.com) or Meander Travel at the Old Port (tel: 26610 37546). Albanian-run Sipa Tours (tel: 26610 56415 or 6976 650713; www.sipatours.com) arranges less frantic, two-, seven- or custom-length tours across southern Albania.

Just beyond, at a tight hairpin turn, are signs pointing down to secluded **Agní** ⑲. Parking at the road's end is limited, so in peak season it's best to arrive at Agní by boat from Nisáki or Kalámi. Agní is known to lots of happy diners, many of whom come here year after year to the three excellent tavernas that sit right on the picturesque beach.

Lawrence Durrell's beloved 'White House' still stands at the far end of **Kalámi** ⑳ bay. It is now part holiday lodgings, part taverna, where you can enjoy the marvellous scenery that inspired him to write *Prospero's Cell* (a hugely evocative read that describes Corfu in the days before tourism) between 1936 and 1939. Despite various vacation villas and an insensitive new hotel complex that defaces one side of the hills enclosing the bay, it remains a fairly tranquil resort.

Charming **Kouloúra** ㉑, one bay north, is scarcely large enough for a handful of fishing boats and a small taverna, but it is one of the most picturesque and photographed corners of Corfu. A constant stream of buses, cars and motorbikes pull up at the large parking space high above on the main road to gaze down on its classic, tiny horseshoe harbour enclosed by tall cypresses. There is not a more typically Ionian view in the archipelago. Gerald Durrell, the brother of Lawrence, lived in Kouloúra and, while there, penned the amusing *My Family and Other Animals*.

Just past Kouloúra, yet another lovely white-pebble beach, far below, beckons invitingly to drivers from the clifftop road. It belongs to **Kerasiá**, an attractive low-key resort with a handful of villas. It is reached by the turn-off to Ágios Stéfanos or, for the energetic, via a 20-minute coastal path from Kouloúra. **Ágios Stéfanos Sinión** is the most exclusive of this coast's beautiful bays.

Kensington-on-Sea

The northeast coast is sometimes dubbed 'Kensington-on-Sea' after the well-heeled British visitors who holiday here.

Kassiópi, a fishing village with a long history, now a thriving resort

Fishing boats and yachts bob lazily in the circular harbour, ringed by whitewashed cottages and tavernas. From here, a minor paved road or another path leads to more exposed **Avláki** bay, the last in line before Kassiópi.

Not so long ago, **Kassiópi** ㉒ was merely a quiet fishing village. These days it's a highly popular little resort. In fact, Kassiópi was a thriving settlement even in Roman times, visited by Cicero, Cato and Emperor Nero, among others. It is named after the god Zeus Kassios, a cult with origins in distant Syria, and the village church supposedly stands on the site of a temple built in his honour. Its successor, the delightful church of Panagía Kassópitra (Our Lady of Kassiópi), used to be the foremost shrine on Corfu before the arrival of St Spyridon. Its icons attest to the many miracles worked here. Opposite the church, the Angevins built a partly ruined medieval fortress during the 13th century to provide shelter for the locals from pirate raids.

Belfry at deserted Paleá Períthia

The town is packed with tourists during midsummer, but the deeply indented harbour is still home to local fishermen. Nightlife is lively and Kassiópi has something of a party image with its tacky tourist bars. However, there are still several passably authentic Greek restaurants. Bathing beaches lie to either side of the resort, especially at Imeroliá, west of the castle headland.

The most spectacular portion of the coast road ends just before Kassiópi; beyond it gentler, shrub-covered foothills border a broad coastal plain blessed with an abundance of hayfields, vines and almond trees. The first sandy beach along this stretch, **Kalamáki**, is actually rather unattractive, as dull as its grey sand. Give it a miss and continue to **Ágios Spyrídon** ❷❸, 3km (2 miles) further northwest, a small but attractive beach with fine golden sand, a taverna and great views across to Albania.

An interesting break from the seaside is provided by the 'ghost town' of **Paleá Períthia** ❷❹ (Old Períthia, sometimes Áno Períthia), set on the northern slopes of Mt Pandokrátor and accessible by a turning opposite the road to Ágios Spyrídon. (Maps showing the road as unpaved are out of date.) Incredibly, Períthia was once the capital of Kassiópi district. Today there are just a handful of families resident in summer, operating a few tavernas with a beautiful view of the crumbling village and the mountain overhead. Simply sitting and savouring the peace and quiet here makes a journey well worthwhile.

No natural disaster overtook Paleá Períthia; its residents simply moved to the coast in search of work during the 1960s and 1970s. Cobbled lanes between the old stone houses, slowly being done up, and churches, provide a haunting glimpse of old Corfiot life. In spring this valley is a great spot for naturalists, who can spot hundreds of butterflies, birds and wild flowers. The long-distance Corfu Trail passes through here, descending from a saddle on the flank of Mt Pandokrátor.

THE NORTH

Corfu's north shore features an 8-km (5-mile) expanse of sand stretching from Cape Róda through Aharávi and beyond to Cape Agía Ekateríni. Although the width of the beach and its sand quality varies, the sea is very shallow for a long way out, making it popular with young families.

From the main highway, a number of side roads go down to **Almyrós** beach, with two holiday complexes. Further on, don't be put off by the roadside sprawl of tourist facilities at **Aharávi** ❷❺. The side roads leading to its long beach are lush with olive and citrus trees, giving this relatively new resort

Sidári's rock formations

much laid-back charm, as does the 'Old Village' on the south side of the road, opposite the water pump.

The neighbouring resort of **Róda** ㉖ quite heavily developed with several older buildings, narrow streets, and a pretty little square still surviving among the tavernas, gift shops and touristy bars and restaurants. The remains of the 5th-century BC Doric temple of Apollo have been discovered here but, despite a signpost, there is nothing to see.

The booming resort of **Sidári** ㉗, 39km (24 miles) from Kérkyra Town by the most direct road, is by far the most developed on the north coast and its main street reflects many of the less savoury aspects of mass tourism on the island. Nonetheless, a picturesque little village square survives, with a charming church. The broad, sandy main beach has very shallow warm water and a wide range of water sports. Sidári's finest feature, however, is the series of striking coastal **rock formations** flanking the resort on the west.

The striated sandstone here is continuously carved by the wind and the sea into sandy coves with caves and ledges (some of which are very good for diving). There are a number of adjacent bays to explore, becoming more spectacular the further west you go. At the last bay you can go no further and, for your own safety, a fence blocks the top of the bluff. The view

Channel of Love

The most famous of Sidári's many rock formations is the Canal d'Amour. Legend has it that anyone who swims through this narrow channel (when the water is in shade, according to some versions) will find the man or woman of their dreams. The problem is that the original Canal d'Amour, topped by a sea arch, collapsed long ago, and today nobody can quite decide which is the 'official' Canal d'Amour. If you are in search of love, take no chances and swim through them all.

from here – of the giant cliffs tumbling straight down into the sea – is breathtaking.

From Sidári (and also from Ágios Stéfanos Gýrou), boat trips run to the three small islets lying to the northwest, known collectively as the **Diapóndia Islands**. Going clockwise, these are Mathráki, Othoní and Eríkoussa, and are famous both for their fish-

Perouládes panorama

ing grounds and fervent Italian patronage. **Othoní** is the largest and most mountainous, and the westernmost point of Greece, and is occasionally visited as a day trip from Ágios Stéfanos only, along with hilly, green **Mathráki**, the smallest islet, but with a long, sandy beach. **Eríkousa** has a pair of excellent sandy beaches and attracts the most visitors, from Sidári especially. Each island has at least one taverna and one place to stay overnight – two or three establishments in the cases of Othoní and Mathráki – but you'll have to reserve well in advance for summer.

Stunning views of the northwestern tip of Corfu await at **Perouládes 28**, 2km (1.2 miles) west of Sidári. Follow signs through the village for **Longás** beach; from the road's-end car park, a flight of steps leads down to this narrow but eminently scenic beach at the base of sheer, gold-grey striated cliffs. There are no facilities on the beach itself, but the restaurant on the clifftop by the top of the stairs provides a fantastic place to watch the sunset. From the village, another track leads out to Cape Drástis, the island's northwestern tip, where you'll discover a pretty cove and more interesting offshore rock formations.

THE NORTHWEST

Ágios Stéfanos Gýrou ㉙ (not to be confused with Ágios Stéfanos Sinión on the east coast), also called San Stefano, is a popular family resort with a long, wide beach of compacted sand and pebbles ending at white cliffs. West of the resort, small boats depart from the fishing harbour to the Diapóndia Islands. From the port, a path leads out onto Cape Kefáli, the westernmost point of Corfu.

A 45-minute clifftop walk to the south (or a roundabout inland drive) leads to **Arílas**, in the next bay. This low-key resort is less developed than its neighbour – perhaps because the gently shelving beach is much smaller and narrower.

Much the finest, and best-protected beach in the far northwest lies beyond yet another headland (Cape Aríla) at **Ágios Geórgios Págon** ㉚: a long (2km/1.2 miles) crescent of coarse sand. Water sports (including scuba diving) are available, and the water is deep and clean. There are stunning views over the bay from the cliffs at Afiónas, a picturesque village on the sheltering headland which ends at a little lighthouse.

Paleokastrítsa

You can reach the most celebrated beauty spot on the island by a fast, paved road from Kérkyra Town; the distance is 25km (16 miles). During the 1820s **Paleokastrítsa** ㉛ was a favourite picnic spot for High Commissioner Sir Frederick Adam, and it is said that he had the first road built across Corfu especially to reach it. (To justify the expense he proposed constructing a military convalescent home there, but it was never built.)

Several small coves with incredibly clear turquoise

Alkinoos's palace

Many claim that Paleokastrítsa was the site of the reputedly fabulous palace of King Alkinoös. Its magnificent setting is indeed fit for a king.

water nestle in a coastline of hills and promontories draped in olive, cypress and lemon trees. Strips of partly sandy, partly shingle beach ring the shoreline, and sea grottoes yawning out of sheer cliffs provide employment for the local boatmen who ferry visitors to and fro. Some way south in the sea, a large ship-shaped rock known as Kolóvri is said to be the petrified Phaeacian ship that once bore Ulysses home.

Paleokastrítsa's monastery

'Paleó', as it is sometimes called, was never a village as such, but merely the port of the hilltown of Lákones. The year-round population is said to be less than 50, but this is hard to believe during the high season, when several hundred Corfiots move down from their hillside homes to cater for the crowds that flock to this scenic spot.

Fortunately, no building has been permitted to crowd the bright little **monastery of Theotókou** (daily 7am–1pm and 3–8pm; free) that perches on the main, wooded promontory. You must dress appropriately to enter, and suitable wraps are provided at the gate for women. Established during the 13th century after the discovery here of an icon of the Virgin Mary, the monastery was rebuilt following a fire in the 17th century. Today it is a lovely, peaceful haven, and many thousands of photographs have been taken of its delightful patio, where a picturesque, creamy-yellow, typically Ionian belltower decked

Pink rocks and deep-blue 'eyes'

with pink bougainvillea is set off by a brilliant blue sky. Its three bells represent the Holy Trinity. Visit in the evening when there are few visitors and the soft light is at its best.

A tiny museum harbours ancient icons, vestments and various oddities, including an old olive press, huge wine barrels, a giant clam and some enormous bones. 'Part of the skeleton of a huge sea monster which was killed by the crew of a French ship in 1860 in the waters by the monastery', enthuses the caption on the latter item. The poor creature was in fact probably a whale. As you enter the monastery church, you may be given a candle to light; a donation, or patronage of the monastery shop, is expected.

Paleó's main beach of Ágios Spyrídon is the most crowded, but the departure point for boat excursions to Corfu's only sea caves and grottoes, with their mysterious pink rocks and blue 'eyes' – extremely deep holes that, with the play of sunlight, turn an incredibly deep blue colour. A longer trip can be made north from Paleokastrítsa to Ágios Geórgios Págon – a beautiful voyage, chugging past jagged cliffs that dwarf your tiny vessel. If you are lucky, you might see the dolphins that often cavort in these waters.

The finest view of Paleokastrítsa is from the precariously perched balcony-village of **Lákones**, high above the coastline. One gets there by a twisty paved road, or a marked path. A little further on, at a café called – with some understatement – Bella Vista, is a magnificent panorama that ranks among the finest in Europe; in pre-café days, this was a favourite picnic spot for High Commissioner Adam and his Corfiot wife.

From Paleokastrítsa ('Little Old Castle') you can see the massive walls of **Angelókastro** ㉜ (Mon–Fri May–Sept 8.30am–3pm, extra hours as funding permits; charge), which may have been built during the 12th century by Byzantine Emperor Manuel I Komnenos; it certainly existed by 1272, when Norman raiders from Sicily took it briefly. In 1537 several thousand Corfiots held out against Ottoman attack in this nearly impregnable citadel. From the car park at the foot of the castle, itself reached via the all-but-empty hamlet of Kríni, it is an easy, 10-minute climb to the summit with its little church of Ágios Ioánnis and some mysterious rock-cut graves adjacent. Little else is left inside the walls beyond some cisterns, but the views from here are marvellous – it was a strategic watchpoint over the sea lanes to Italy, and in visual communication with Kérkyra Town's Old Fort.

The huge Angelókastro fortress

Backtrack through Kríni to **Makrádes** ㉝, where the main road is lined with souvenir stalls and tavernas catering to tour buses. The village itself (off a side road to the left) is a brightly whitewashed cluster of houses with many picturesque corners. Just beyond Makrádes, follow the steep, but completely paved road to **Pági**. The first reward is the stunning vista of Ágios Geórgios Bay you get before you arrive. The second is the peaceful mountain village itself, crowned by an Ionian belfry.

Alternatively, you can join the main trans-island road at the **Troumbétas Pass**. *Troumbétas* means 'trumpet', and the pass is so called after the musically minded officer in charge of the road construction team who liked to stand on the pass above and blow his trumpet to call the crew to lunch. From here you can head north to Sidári or Róda, or return to Kérkyra Town via Skriperó.

THE WEST

The wide Rópa Valley opens out just inland from Paleokastrítsa and its gateway village of Gardeládes. This former marsh was drained by the Italians during their brief occupation in World War II, and is now the island's agricultural heartland. South of Rópa, along the west coast, lie Corfu's best beaches, with wide stretches of deep, golden sand.

The Rópa river flows down through the valley and out to the sea at **Érmones**, making it the main contender for the site where Odysseus was found by Nausika and her retinue. The bay is picturesque, but its small (100m/330ft wide) beach of sand and pebble is not particularly attractive and is hemmed in by hotel and bungalow developments. The main hotel runs a somewhat rickety funicular service down to the beach.

By contrast, **Myrtiótissa** ❸❹ was described by Lawrence Durrell, over 70 years ago, as 'perhaps the loveliest beach in the world', but today it is perhaps the most overrated beach on Corfu. Although the access road (signposted at Kelliá village, near Pélekas) is now paved, it is still dauntingly steep as it worms its way down forested cliffs, and

Glyfáda's long sandy beach, one of the finest on the west coast

except in spring or autumn, parking is hopeless (there is a car-park of sorts up by the handy Bella Vista taverna, and the local monastery, as well as turning leeway). Most days, the beach is a diamond-shaped lozenge of sand at best 40m (130ft) broad, with offshore boulders to baffle the waves and several drink, trinket and umbrella stalls compounding the space problem. It's usually wall-to-wall, uniformly naked bodies here, as this is the island's designated naturist cove – perhaps rather scandalously more or less in full view of the 14th-century **monastery of Myrtiótissa**, uphill to the north (open 8am–1pm and 5–9pm, but doorbell not always answered).

Adjacent to Myrtiótissa as the seagull flies, but via a roundabout land route, is a beach more worthy of acclaim, **Glyfáda** ㉟. Against a backdrop of crumbling cliffs with rock formations at either end, this 450-metre stretch of sand is one of the finest on the island, and accordingly popular with day trippers from Kérkyra Town and other resorts – as well as many Greeks and Italians in July. Swimming is superb; the water is initially shallow, but deepens further out. There is often a bit of surf for boogie boarders, as well as periodic strong undertow at the northern end (as on many beaches along the west coast). Glyfáda is somewhat overwhelmed by two large hotel complexes, but there's no arguing with the four-star sand and amenities (including showers, sunbeds and water sports).

A steep hill leads up from Glyfáda to the village of **Pélekas** ㊱. Today it is busy and commercialised, full of travel agencies, restaurants, cafés and rooms for rent. Nonetheless, it is still an attractive place and makes a good coffee or meal stop – if you can find a parking place. Follow signposts to the famous **Kaiser's Throne**, just above Pélekas on a high ridge. At this panoramic viewpoint, Kaiser Wilhelm built a small telescope point to watch the spectacular sunsets. From here, at certain times of the year, the sun appears to slide diagonally down the hillside and into the sea. The views at any time are excellent, from Paleokastrítsa in the west to Kérkyra Town in the east.

The closest beach to Pelekás, well signposted below the village, is **Kondogialós**, reached by yet another steep, winding access road. It's actually longer than Glyfáda, at about 700m (2,275ft), though the beach is a bit narrower, with a portion of rocky shore providing good snorkelling in crystal waters. Wooden boardwalks cross the burning sand, and there's some free parking available at the far north end (most west-coast beaches have unavoidable, stiff parking fees collected by roving wardens). Development comprises a handful of tavernas and a large hillside hotel complex.

The unspoiled hill town of **Sinarádes** ㊲ lies 5km (3 miles) south of Pélekas. Towards the north end of Sinarádes, opposite the Venetian-style church tower, signs point up a stair street to the **History and Folklore Museum of Central Corfu** (Mon–Sat 9am–2pm; charge). This minimally restored traditional Corfiot house, of a type prevalent between 1860 and 1960, contains two floors crammed with artefacts and documents. The ground floor has been left more or less as it was when inhabited, with cooking and hearth implements in the kitchen plus mocked-up salon and bedroom. The star of the single room top-floor gallery, mostly devoted to farming and craft tools (including a shoemaker's workbench), is a portion of

Sinarádes

a *papyrélla* raft, made of cane fennel, used along the west and northwest coasts of Corfu until World War II. Other oddities include a moray eel trap, a wicker cage to keep toddlers from wandering off, and two special saddles used by village women when giving birth.

The scenic bay of **Ágios Górdis** ㊳, enclosed by shaggy slopes (but rather dominated by the giant Pink Palace backpackers' complex), is punctuated by a massive pinnacle rising from the water at the southern end – an excellent spot for snorkelling, as are the rocks at the northern end. The 600-metre sand-and-shingle beach, despite being far from the best on Corfu, can get crowded in season, as the resort just inland is sizable.

EXCURSIONS

Both the idyllic island of Paxí (the ancient Paxos) and the nearby Greek mainland are easily accessible for day trips out of Kérkyra Town, Kávos and Benítses. Corfu travel agents can provide you with information on such excursions and on ferry schedules if you wish to stay longer.

Paxí

One of the most delightful island experiences in the Mediterranean awaits you just 10 nautical miles south of Corfu. Tiny, verdant **Paxí** ㊴, the smallest of the seven principal Ionian Islands – approximately 11km (7 miles) long and 5km (3 miles) wide – has some 300,000 olive trees and about 2,400 permanent residents. It is famous for the quality of its olive oil; to this day Paxí earns almost as much from olives as from tourism. This quiet, relatively uncommercialised island is wonderfully tidy – there is virtually no litter or roadside rubbish, while houses, villas, shops and restaurants are maintained and painted as if in preparation for a competition for the best-kept Greek island.

The clear, limpid waters off Paxí are irresistible. The island has no natural sandy beaches, though off the shingle strip at Lákka the bottom is pure sand. However, you'll find excellent swimming from flat rocks and numerous pebbly coves around

A Chip off the Old Block

According to Greek mythology, the sea god Poseidon created Paxí by striking off the southern part of Corfu to make a retreat for himself and his mistress, Amphitriti. Kirki (Circe), the enchantress who in Homer's Odyssey detained Ulysses on her island and turned his men into swine, supposedly came from Paxí.

Pretty Lákka on Paxí

the shoreline, even if many are accessible only by boat. There is a small strip of imported sand on the islet of Mogonísi in the far south, but it is nearly always crowded.

Sea caves in the towering cliffs along the west coast are truly spectacular, and the blue water there is so dazzling in its intensity that snorkelling is something you won't soon forget. The sea depth off these sheer rocks plunges from 25m to 90m (82ft to 295ft), with fish of varying sizes gliding along in schools, at different levels. The largest of these caves, Ypapandí, was said to be a lair of Poseidon. A modern legend has it that a British submarine hid here for many months during World War II, venturing out on occasion to conduct its valiant operations. Soaring out of the sea along this stunning coast is **Orthólithos** – a huge finger of rock that has been hewn out of the cliff face by the elements.

Peaceful Paxí often appeals to those who want to get away from it all. But this can be difficult in midsummer, especially in the first three weeks of August, when the tiny island becomes a magnet for Italian tourists. Then, prices swell accordingly and accommodation is heavily booked. The island has only two large hotel complexes; other accommodation is in fairly upmarket villas and apartments, though visitors who want to stay only a few nights can often find rooms to rent in private houses. However, in high season it's sensible to book well in advance.

As a day tripper, you normally get a whistle-stop tour of Paxí (including its seacaves) and Andípaxi, where you don't even go ashore – boats merely anchor for a swim. To do Paxí justice, you should visit on a scheduled ferry and plan to stay at least two nights – enough time to see all the island's highlights and savour its relaxed atmosphere.

From Kérkyra Town, ferries to Paxí all go via Igoumenítsa, but schedules change frequently so enquire at the ferry agencies.

The harbour at Gáïos

The journey takes up to three hours (via Igoumenítsa). There are also one-day excursions combining Paxí and Párga (*see page 80*). In the high season there is sometimes a separate *kaïki* service between Gáïos and Párga, taking around 75 minutes.

All boats arrive at **Gáïos**, the small quayside capital of the island. The pretty waterfront square is lined with taver-

Beach on Andípaxi

nas, shops and charming weathered houses, while handsome yachts fill the harbour.

Any tour of this tiny island will also take in the delightful coastal villages of Lákka and Longós. **Lákka** is a pretty port situated around an almost landlocked bay on the northern island shore, ideal for water sports. It's the island's sailing capital and has several cafés and tavernas. From Lákka there is a pleasant walk to a lighthouse on the cliffs and – a bit further – to the inland monastery of **Ypapandí**, the oldest on the island, whose belltower provides scenic views.

Longós (also spelled Loggós) is a quieter fishing village huddled around a lovely harbour. Here, too, you'll find numerous places to eat and drink. Two of the best Paxian beaches – Levréhio and Monodéndri – are also near here.

There is a regular bus service between the three main settlements, though it operates only during the day and early evening. Scooter hire is available. There are a handful of taxis, but it can be difficult (if not impossible) to find one late at night.

Walking around the island is an attractive option. Little-used tracks and paths along stone terraces and through mature olive groves end in idyllic hamlets. Along the roadsides you'll see abandoned stone cottages and old olive presses, as well as lovingly tended grape arbours, cacti and bougainvillea in profusion. The surrounding hillsides are dotted with round stone towers of ruined, mastless windmills.

A popular walk leads from Magaziá, in the centre of the island, up to the tidy hilltop cemetery at the Ágii Apóstoli (Holy Apostles) Church, where there is a striking view of the chalk-coloured Erimítis cliffs.

Andípaxi

Andípaxi ④ (Antipaxos) is an undeveloped island less than three nautical miles south of Gáïos; by shuttle-boat the journey takes 30 to 40 minutes. Cloaked in vineyards and lapped by transparent turquoise water, Andípaxi has only a handful of permanent residents but attracts plenty of visitors who converge on the island's two beaches. Little Vríka cove boasts an arc of fine, white sand, with tavernas at either end and a few beach umbrellas for hire. The nearby bay of Vatoúmi has brilliant-white pebbles along its coastal strip but a soft, sandy bottom underwater; there's one taverna on the hillside, plus a newer one behind the beach.

Swimming at both Vríka and Vatoúmi is superb, but don't expect to enjoy them in solitude. Excursion *kaïkia* continually drop off bathers throughout the day, and numerous private boats also moor offshore. In high season, these sweet little beaches are often sadly overpopulated.

Giant tree

Between Magaziá and Fondána stands the island's largest olive tree – it takes five men with outstretched arms to embrace the huge twisted trunk. This giant stands in an incredible grove of 500-year-old trees, all still producing fruit faithfully every two years.

Párga

Párga ④ village occupies an exquisite seascape on mainland Greece's northwest coast, just east of Paxí. Its several consecutive bays are backed by verdant hillsides and dotted by offshore islands. As you arrive by sea, watch for the tiny island of Panagía, just off Kryonéri beach, crowned by a lonely church.

Like Corfu, this is by no means 'untouched Greece'. Párga has been very commercialised for many years, with a profusion of restaurants,

Párga harbour

bars and tourist shops, none terribly different from those in Corfu. Yet, even after the picturesque, quiet appeal of Paxí (excursion boats may visit the two in succession, so comparison is inevitable), Párga is still a delight. Its spectacular setting and views and quiet narrow whitewashed streets have an appeal all their own.

A Venetian castle built around 1400 on an earlier Norman structure looms above the promontory immediately to the north of the town. The climb up Párga's steep streets to the castle is actually shorter than it looks from below and well worth the effort for the stupendous views. Be sure to follow the lanes around the base of the castle-hill for additional views of the next bay, **Váltos**, fringed by a long, splendid golden-sand beach.

If you have a day or two to spend in Párga, take the popular boat trip up the River Ahérondas (Acheron), thought to be the mythological River Styx – the gateway to the Underworld. It concludes at the **Nekromanteion**, the Oracle of the Dead. Here, in a subterranean chamber, the ancient Greeks sought contact with the souls of the departed, under the auspices of the local priests of Hades, the Lord of the Underworld.

WHAT TO DO

SHOPPING

Greece is now one of the more expensive Mediterranean destinations, so don't expect great bargains on Corfu – except perhaps during the August sales. In souvenir shops you might find that some good-natured bargaining is tolerated if you are buying more than one item or spending a reasonable amount – but don't push it. Local profit margins have to cover not only the tourist months but also the off-season, when most shops are closed, and some shops even put up signs saying 'Fixed Prices' or 'No Bargaining'.

If you are not a resident of the EU, you might be able to claim back the 23 percent VAT (sales tax) included in the price, but only if you spend over €120 in one day at a shop participating in the scheme – there are rather few of these on Corfu.

Where to Shop

By far the best range and quality of goods on the island are to be found in Kérkyra Town. Here, the elegant old-world atmosphere of evening shopping (even if you are only window-browsing) is not to be missed. There are also a number of specialist outlets on the road from Kérkyra Town to Paleokastrítsa or Róda. These are worth a visit, particularly the no-name olive-wood workshop just below Skriperó (look for the logs and power saws outside at the front).

Best Buys

Gifts from the olive tree. Corfu's most plentiful commodity – olive-wood prunings – provides the basis for many fine

Taking it easy

souvenirs. Local artisans carve attractive bowls, platters, trays, utensils, statuettes, jewellery, toys and all sorts of other ingenious olive-wood oddities. The island's olives, olive paste and high-quality olive oil are appreciated worldwide, and a small bar of olive-oil soap, often tastefully gift wrapped, is an ideal, inexpensive present.

Pottery and ceramics. Corfu is home to many talented potters. You'll come across some lovely ceramics, including museum copies (the shop in the Old Fort in Kérkyra Town specialises in the latter).

Gold and silver. Silversmiths still create bowls and trays using centuries-old Greek and Venetian patterns, beating out the silver much as their ancestors would have done. Many of the jewellery designs are based on archetypal symbols from the earliest years of of Greek civilisation, including the lion, dolphin, ram and bull. Evgeníou Voulgáreos Street, off the Listón,

Corfiot villages produce handmade lace and embroidery

is the place to find silver in Kérkyra Town.

Leather. Leather is one of the few areas where prices are advantageous on Corfu. Handbags, sandals, shoes, gloves wallets and belts are often very good buys in Kérkyra Town. Agíon Pándon Street is home to many young and creative fashion designers; more traditional outlets are found on Nikifórou Theotókou.

Icons for sale

Weaving and embroidery. There's a good selection of handwoven and embroidered items. Colourful woollen shoulder bags called *tagária*, handwoven floor mats in muted colours, tablecloths, napkins, aprons, skirts and blouses of lace and cotton (in particular those woven in Corfiot villages) are always popular. The best buys in this category are probably cotton needlework shawls and bedspreads. The village of Kassiópi is home to a traditional industry of lace and crocheted goods.

Reproduction icons. These are on sale all over Kérkyra Town and vary greatly in price according to size and quality. Icons are also sold at the monasteries at Mt Pandokrátor and Paleokastrítsa.

Other specialities. Kumquat liqueur is a novelty made from a small southeast Asian citrus fruit grown on Corfu (locally spelled as koum quat). There are medium and dry varieties of this sweet, orange-coloured drink, though the clear extract is considered the best quality. It is sold throughout Corfu, and the Mavromatis factory on the Paleokastrítsa road is a popular stop with tour groups. You can also sample crystallised kumquat fruits.

Another particularly sweet treat worth trying is nougat of almonds or sugared nuts (*mandoláto*). In addition, the rich island flora ensures that its famous honey always possesses a distinctive character. In the fruit and vegetable markets, look for bags of herbs and spices.

Although not ranked amongst the better Greek DOCs, Corfu does produce wine of quaffable quality, and you can purchase a number of bottled local brands, for example from the Theotoky Estate near Giannádes. Other drinks available include *oúzo* (the national aperitif) and Greek brandy, particularly Metaxa, rated from three to seven stars according to quality and strength.

Other typically Greek souvenir ideas include strands of worry beads (*kombologiá*); CDs of quality Greek music (best for this is Ihos 65, at Agíon Pándon 4, near the Listón); or a *bríki*, a long-stemmed copper coffee pot used for making Greek coffee, which also makes an attractive ornament.

ENTERTAINMENT

Corfu is indeed a very musical island. Thanks to the Venetian legacy, Kérkyra Town alone boasts three orchestras, with nearly a dozen more spread over the island, representing several hundred musicians in all, as well as a municipal choir and a chamber-music group; it is claimed that nearly half the Athens Symphony Orchestra is Corfu Conservatory-trained. Marching brass bands (the somewhat confusingly called *filarmonikés orhístres*) are a regular fixture at festivals, and often give summer Sunday concerts on the Spianáda. Despite current funding problems, summer still sees some festivals, notably the Ágios Ioánnis soul, rock and folk festival (www.agiotfest. co.uk) and Paleokastrítsa's Varkarola Festival in mid-August.

Theatre lovers might attend summer performances (often of ancient Greek plays), either in one of Kérkyra Town's two

The Corfiots' love of music runs deep

fortresses or at the Mon Repos outdoor theatre. Other venues for quality events include the auditorium of the Ionian Academy, the somewhat grim Municipal Theatre (a replacement for the one bombed in September 1943), the New Fort, 7Arts (Epta Technon Topos) in Víros near the airport, and Lucciola Bar-Bistro in Sgómbou. For details of all concerts, festivals and theatre pick up a cultural events leaflet from the airport or the local tourist information office. The website www.corfuwhatson.com is also very useful, as are posters announcing village *panigýria* during the summer.

Authentic performances of songs and dances occur at village festivals throughout the season, with both young and old dressed in the traditional costumes of their ancestors. Otherwise, Kérkyra Town hosts 'Cultural Evenings' on Tuesdays during summer, at Platía Dimarhíou, Platía Ionikí and the Old Port plaza in Spiliá, featuring folk dancing, classical music and traditional choral music.

For less formal happenings, look no further than the nearest musical bar or dance club in any major resort like Kávos or Sidári – though in these tough times the emphasis is more on small, often weekends-only spots like DiZi Beach Bar at Érmones, the Stablus complex on Solomoú below the New Fort, or Café del Arte on Kandoúni Bízi in Kérkyra Town. The formerly lively mega-nightclub strip along the main road (Ethnikís Andistáseos) west of the New Port has pretty much withered away since the 2010–11 Greek debt crisis, but a likely survivor there is Au Bar (www.aubarcorfu.com) at no. 34.

Corfiot Easter

Kérkyra Town stages the most colourful Easter (Páskha) celebration in Greece. Here it is often called Lambrí ('brilliance'), and the spectacle attracts throngs of Athenians and other mainlanders, with all town hotels full for the duration. Every church has its Good Friday procession of the *epitáfios* or funeral bier of Christ. The best starts after nightfall, departing from the cathedral with the bishop, dignitaries and Corfu's famous 'philharmonic' (brass) bands.

On Holy Saturday morning, the body of the patron saint, Spyridon, is paraded at length around town in honour of his miraculous intervention in 1553, which saved Corfu from famine. Then, at 11am, police clear the streets. Suddenly pottery, old plates, vases and other breakables are hurled from the upper storeys of houses. The best explanation of this old and unique Corfu custom is that it banishes misfortune, including Judas' betrayal of Jesus.

The Catholic Easter Saturday eve mass takes place somewhat before the Orthodox one. At midnight, when the Orthodox bishop intones *'Hristós anésti'* ('Christ is risen'), every electric light goes on, fireworks soar overhead, church bells ring and – most memorably – everyone lights a candle. On Easter Sunday at noon, lambs are put to the spit, wine flows like water and men perform traditional Greek and Corfiot dances.

The island has one casino, which is set to move to the Corfu Palace Hotel in early 2012 (anticipated hours 8pm–2am; formal dress code; minimum age 18). It offers roulette, blackjack, baccarat and chemin de fer.

Greek Nights

During your stay you will probably come across a 'Greek Night', though these are not nearly as widespread as formerly; they generally comprise of a traditional

Easter procession

meal (more or less), Corfiot music (usually live) and dancing, touted as the main attraction. Traditional Corfiot and national Greek dances are taught from an early age, and the dancers – whether specially hired performers, restaurant staff or simply locals doing their bit – can almost always be relied on for an energetic performance.

Corfiot men revel in athletic, fast dances with high-kicking steps and not a little bravado. Dancing in a ring of fire to the accompaniment of plate smashing is quite typical. Another stunt involves picking up a glass of wine with the mouth from a press-up position. The wine is downed with a jerk of the neck; more macho types bite a chunk out of the empty glass before tossing it contemptuously aside. Another crowd pleaser has a dancer bending back to apparently pick up a heavy table only with his teeth (he's actually taking the table's weight on his chest and stomach.) Expert practitioners extend this feat to a table with a chair on top, and some go for broke by getting a young child to sit on the chair.

Renting a boat

The best way to enjoy the coastline is by boat. You can rent all types of motorboats, from a small outboard to a 10m (33ft) *caique*.

By the end of the evening, the dancers will probably have cajoled everyone onto the floor to join in a version of the *syrtáki*, Greece's best-known line dance; steps are simplified for visitors.

Accompaniment is usually provided by a *bouzoúki*, which for many foreigners has become synonymous with all Greek music. In fact, the instrument (of Middle Eastern origin) is a very recent import to the island, though the popular melodies of Manos Hatzidakis, Mikis Theodorakis and the great composers of *rebétika* have made it an intrinsic part of Greek – and Corfiot – folklore.

SPORTS AND RECREATION

Snorkelling and diving. A clear, salubrious sea laps the island's innumerable rocky inlets, and you will find small, fascinating grottoes and offshore rocks near Paleokastrítsa, Sidári and Perouládes. Paleokastrítsa is considered to be one of Europe's best diving locations, though the water can be chilly year-round, and per-dive prices are expensive by Mediterranean standards. Don't be put off by Neptune grass at certain east-coast points; beds of the plant (*Posidonia oceanica*) serve as a nursery and browsing ground for some of the most colourful fish, and indicate lack of pollution.

All scuba-diving schools have qualified instructors who will choose dive locations according to the amount of experience you have. Extended boat trips are available for advanced divers. For the more advanced trips, or to hire equipment on your own, you will need to show an appropriate diving certificate. West-coast schools to single out include Diving Fun Club at Ágios Geórgios Págon (www.corfudivingfunclub.

gr); Achilleon Diving Center at Paleokástritsa and Érmones (www.diving-corfu.com); and Korfu Diving at Ambelákia cove, Paleokastrítsa (www.korfudiving.com).

Water sports. Dassiá and Ýpsos are established water-sports centres, and along with Kalámi are some of the few locations where waterskiing (in decline) is still practiced. Windsurfing equipment is available for hire at every beach on the island where the right conditions prevail, and instruction is offered at many places, in particular Surf4Fun at Íssos (www.surf4fun-korfu.de). Parasailing is available at several beaches, as is kite-surfing; there's a dedicated kite school at Halikoúnas beach (www.kite-club-korfu.com).

Golf. The acclaimed Corfu Golf Club (tel: 26610 94220), in the Rópa Valley near Érmones, is rated as one of the best in the Mediterranean. The 18-hole course features water hazards and a design that provide a real challenge for seasoned golfers. You can arrange lessons with qualified pros (it's best to book ahead); clubs and other essentials are available for hire. You'll also find a good shop and clubhouse with a bar and restaurant.

A range of motorboats are available to rent

Horse riding. There are two bona fide stables on the island: Rópa Valley Riding Stables (same phone number as the golf course), offering one- to two-hour rides, and Trailriders in Áno Korákiana (www.trailriders.corfu.com), offering two-hour morning or evening rides Monday to Saturday in season.

Cricket. Cricket was introduced by the English and is now an integral part of Corfu's summer scene. Matches take place in the new cricket ground at Gouviá Marina on Saturday and Sunday afternoons, usually attracting enthusiastic spectators. Corfu clubs frequently play against visiting teams from Britain and Malta, among others, and are often participants in the European Cricket Championship (ECC), contested at various venues across Europe between May and August. There is another pitch at the Rópa Golf Club, while youth teams play at the pitch on the Spianáda in Kérkyra Town. Keen cricketers might be able to play with one of the Corfu teams (tel: 26610 47753).

ACTIVITIES FOR CHILDREN

Corfu is a very popular holiday spot for families, and most newer resorts are designed with children in mind. Many larger hotels have separate, shallow children's swimming pools and play areas, and most of the more luxurious hotels have limited-hour crêches and/or 'kids' clubs' with a full range of activities.

While most beaches are perfectly safe for children, those with sandy shores and/or very shallow water will appeal most to families with very young children. These include Róda, Sidári, Aharávi, Arílas, Moraïtika, Mesongí and Kávos, though the latter is also known for its decadent nightlife.

Kérkyra Town is largely for adults, but kids might enjoy a ride in the colourful 19th-century horsedrawn carriages. The *Kalypso Star* glass-bottomed boat leaves the Old Port hourly (11am–6pm) in season for a trip around Vídos Island, where domesticated sea lions perform for the passengers. In Paleokastrítsa the short boat trip to the caves and grottoes is also a winner with kids.

The most popular children's day out (and a great day for all splashaholics) is at the Aqualand water park (www.

aqualand-corfu.com), with many thrill rides, the gentle 'Lazy River', the bouncy castle, swimming pools and special children's play area. Located at Ágios Ioánnis, in the centre of the island some 12km (7.5 miles) west of Kérkyra Town, the park is open daily from May to October. It's quite expensive, but children under four are admitted free and there are reduced rates after 3pm. Special buses make the trip from all over the island. A rival, cheaper water park – Hydropolis – has opened at Aharávi.

If your children love nature and horses, take them pony-trekking, a good outing for the whole family. This can be booked through most tourist agencies.

Most children love 'Greek Night' entertainment, with whirling dancers, rings of fire, smashing plates, tables picked up with teeth and other denture-defying acts. Most tend to start at around 10pm.

Corfu has many beaches suited to young children

Calendar of Events

Celebrations surrounding Carnival and Easter are held on moveable dates between late February and early May. Village festivals occur from May through August.

1 January St Basil's Day (Agíou Vassilíou, Protohroniá). At midnight on New Year's Eve, adults play cards for money and a cake with a lucky coin baked into it (the vassilópita) is cut.

6 January Epiphany (Ta Ágia Theofánia or Ta Fóta). In seaside parishes the priest or bishop blesses the waters by throwing a crucifix into the sea; young men dive competitively to retrieve it.

February Apókries. Carnival Season of three weekends, prior to Lent. Fancy-dress parties, parades with floats and marching bands, and (on the third Sunday), the trial and cremation of 'King Carnival'.

'Clean Monday' First day of Orthodox Lent (Katharí Deftéra). In good weather everyone goes out for a picnic and kite-flying.

8 March St Theodora Augusta (Agía Theodóra Avgoústa). The saint's relics are carried in a procession around Kérkyra Town.

25 March Greek Independence Day: procession in Kérkyra Town.

Good Friday Biers from many churches process through Kérkyra Town.

Easter Saturday Procession of St Spyridon's coffin around Kérkyra Town.

Easter Sunday Fireworks and noisy celebrations with music and dance.

1 May May Day/Labour Day. Workers' parades and excursions to the countryside to gather flowers and greenery for May wreaths.

21 May Ionian Union Day (Énosis ton Eptaníson) marks the anniversary of the seven islands joining Greece in 1864.

17 July Agía Marína. Festivities at Avliótes, Benítses, Sparterá and in San Rocco Square, Kérkyra Town.

11 August Feast day in honour of St Spyridon in Kérkyra Town, including procession of St Spyrídon's coffin.

15 August Kímisis tis Panagías (Dormition of the Virgin); festivals.

First Sunday in November Procession of St Spyridon's coffin.

12 December St Spyridon Day (Agíou Spyrídonos). Everyone named Spyros has open house for friends on their name day.

EATING OUT

Take an idyllic waterside setting, add charcoal-grilled fish, meat on a spit and a crisp salad, and you have the basic components of a typical Greek meal. Olive oil, tomatoes, onion, garlic, cheese and lemon are all essentials of a simple cuisine, though Corfu – owing largely to its Venetian heritage – has a few more elaborate dishes unique to the island, and unusually for Greece local cooking features spicy recipes.

The true *estiatório*, restaurants where pre-cooked dishes have equal or superior billing to grilled items, are common only in Kérkyra Town; in these places it's still customary to inspect simmering casseroles on the range and point to your choice. In the resorts, the taverna – with mostly outdoor

Al fresco dining along the long beach at Ýpsos

Chicken kebab

seating, and thus usually shut from late October to early May – reigns supreme, and ordering by sight is not the rule. But neither should you rely on menus – many of these are wishful thinking, issued free to the establishment by a sponsoring drinks company, listing dishes that are never offered. The only reliable bill of fare will be recited by your waiter; check the menu only to verify prices. These include service charge, but diners normally leave 5 to 10 percent extra for the waiter. An obligatory cover charge includes bread, which varies in quality – darker village bread is excellent.

Corfiots, like most Greeks, enjoy their food warm rather than piping hot. Casserole dishes such as *moussakás* are cooked for lunchtime and either kept warm all day or just reheated at night. If you like your food hot or if you are concerned about the hygiene implications of re-heating, order only grilled dishes in the evening.

Islanders have lunch between 2.30 and 4pm, dinner from 9.30pm onwards, with many establishments taking last orders as late as 11.30pm. Resort tavernas aimed at foreigners begin dinner service at around 7pm; you will have your choice of table then, but the atmosphere is definitely better later.

WHAT TO EAT

Fast Food

For snacks or even lunch, pop into a bakery for a *tyrópita* (cheese-filled *filo* pastry pie); the *filo*-less version looking like a turnover, called *kouroú*, is less messy and more cheese-filled; if it's stuffed with spinach, it's a *spanakópita*.

Varied cuisine

If you tire of local fare, you can usually find everything from gourmet cuisine to ethnic fare, from Chinese stir-fry to crêpes. Don't turn your nose up at Italian food in particular – the Greeks love pizza and pasta, and the large number of Italian visitors demand high standards in summer.

Another cheap takeaway option is *gýros*, better known to western Europeans as *doner kebab*. Pressed pork is sliced off a vertically rotating spit and stuffed into *píta* bread with some garnish, *tzatzíki* and a handful of chips. Alternatively there is *souvláki*: charcoal-grilled cubes of pork or lamb served in the same fashion. *Souvláki* is also served as a main sit-down course in tavernas.

Appetisers

Carefully selected appetisers (*orektiká*) can constitute a full meal. Shared by the whole table, they are a fun way to eat – you have as little or as much as you want and keep ordering until you have had your fill.

The most common appetisers are *tzatzíki*, a yoghurt dip flavoured with garlic, cucumber and mint; *dolmádes*, vine leaves stuffed with rice, onions and herbs– rarely mince – which can be served hot (with egg-lemon sauce) or cold (with yoghurt); *taramosaláta*, cod-roe paste blended with breadcrumbs, olive oil and lemon juice; *skordaliá*, garlic-and-potato sauce served with fried vegetable slices or battered fish; *melitzanosaláta*, a purée of grilled aubergine, onions, olive oil and garlic; *mavromátika*, black-eyed peas; *tyrokafterí*, a spicy cheese dip; and *hórta*, boiled wild greens. *Saganáki* is hard cheese coated in breadcrumbs and then fried, though confusingly the term can also mean a cheese-based red sauce used over mussels and shrimp.

Greek salad or *horiátiki saláta* (usually translated as 'village salad') consists of tomato, cucumber, onion, green peppers and olives topped with feta cheese. Cruets of olive oil and wine vinegar are found with other condiments on the table.

Fish and Seafood

The seas around Corfu have been overfished and prices for fresh fare are likely to shock many visitors. These are often quoted by weight, so to avoid any unpleasant surprises at the end of your meal, watch the fish being weighed (uncleaned) and confirm the weight to avoid fiddles. If the seafood is frozen or farmed (very likely from June to September), this must by law be stated on the menu

Grilled seafood

– though often only in the Greek-language column, or simply with an asterisk.

Larger fish is usually grilled and smaller fish fried. The most common big species, served with fresh lemon and *ladolémono* (olive oil with lemon juice), are listed in our menu reader, *see page 104*; watch out also for several tasty varieties of bream, such as *melanoúri* (saddled bream) or *sargós* (white bream). *Barboúni* (red mullet) is also a popular fish on Corfu, while *fangrí* (large bream), and *synagrída* (dentex) are expensive treats.

Marídes (picarel), *gávros* (anchovy) and *sardélles* (sardines) are served crisp-fried, as are *kalamarákia* (baby squid). More elaborate seafood dishes include *okhtapódi krasáto*, octopus stewed in red wine and tomato sauce; *soupiá* (cuttlefish) with spinach-rice; or *garídes* (prawns) in saganáki sauce.

A Corfiot seafood speciality is piquant *bourdéto*: white-fleshed fish stewed with tomatoes, hot red pepper, onions, garlic and olive oil. *Biánko* is, as the name sugggests, a 'white' (tomato-less) fish stew with lots of garlic, potatoes, white wine, lemon, oil, black pepper and onions.

Meat and Casserole Dishes

Sit-down barbecued dishes include whole chickens or *kondosoúvli* (rotisseried pork). If you want a basic pork or veal cutlet, ask for *brizóla*; lamb chops, however, are *païdákia*.

The Greeks love lamb. *Kléftiko* is oven-roasted lamb, though in Corfu the dish might be served in a sauce of wine, vegetables and yoghurt. Another popular lamb dish is *arní frikassé*, stewed with green vegetables. Even more common is *stámna*: lamb or beef baked in a clay vessel with cinnamon, cloves, sweet pepper and mixed vegetables.

Greece's most famous slow-cooked oven dish is probably *moussakás* – sliced layers of potato, aubergine and minced beef topped with a generous layer of béchamel sauce. It should be firm but succulent, and aromatic with nutmeg; good restaurants make a fresh batch daily. Other common casseroles include *kokinistó* or *stifádo*, braised meat – beef or rabbit – with baby onions.

Sofríto is a Corfiot speciality comprising slices of beef or veal stewed in a sauce of white wine, garlic and wine vinegar with a touch of black pepper and parsley.

Pasta Dishes

Corfiots are very fond of pasta. *Pastítsio* (macaroni pie) is just that, a mixture of macaroni with mince, spices and bechamel sauce. *Giouvétsi* is meat (usually lamb) and *kritharáki* pasta (identical to Italian *orzo*), baked in a clay casserole. Don't confuse *pastítsio* with the local *pastitsáda*, which is either cockerel or lobster chunks in richly flavoured sauce atop thick, round, brown noodles.

Melitzánes imám

Vegetables

Vegetarians should usually find *hórta* (spinach-like wild greens); *gígandes* (giant butter beans) in sauce; or *fasolákia* (string/runner beans) on menus. For a more substantial hot meatless dish, *gemistá* are tomatoes or peppers stuffed with herb-flavoured rice (though meat stock may be used); alternatively, *melitzánes imám* (aubergine stuffed richly with tomato, onions and oil) is reliably vegetarian, as is *briám* or *tourloú* (a ratatouille of aubergines, potatoes and courgettes). Particularly Corfiot is *tsigarélli*, greens (preferably wild) sautéed with hot chilli powder and other spices.

Desserts

Most tavernas bring a plate of seasonal fresh fruit as a finale to your meal; Corfu's magnificent wild strawberries *(fráoules)* are harvested in May and June. However, during summer the only fruits that appear on the restaurant table are Persian melons, watermelons and grapes.

For something more unhealthily sweet, the *zaharoplastío* (sticky-cake shop, mostly in Kérkyra Town) offer incredibly decadent oriental sweets: *baklavás*, layers of honey-soaked filo pastry with walnuts; *kataïfi*, 'shredded wheat' filled with chopped almonds and honey; *galaktoboúreko*, custard pie; or *ravaní*, honey-soaked sponge cake. If you prefer dairy desserts, try yoghurt topped with local honey (*méli*); *kréma* (custard), or *ryzógalo*, cold rice pudding. *Loukoumádes* are puffy deep-fried dough balls dipped in syrup, often sold by street vendors.

WHAT TO DRINK

Alcoholic Drinks

Corfu produces a reasonable quantity of wine, but much of this is kept back for private use. Usually light red (*kokkinéli*) or deep purple in colour, it is best drunk cool from the cellar. It ranges in quality from almost undrinkable to good-value tippling; approach with caution, a half-litre to start with.

Among local bottled wines, the most expensive is Theotoki, a somewhat fruity white produced solely from

Oúzo

vineyards in the Rópa Valley. Otherwise, choose from the range of mainland Greek wines. Three top-drawer, medium-priced reds are Ktima Papaïoannou, Tsantali Rapsani and almost anything from Nemea. For a premium white, try Gentilini Robola from neighbouring Kefaloniá, Spyropoulos, Tselepos and Skouras from the Peloponnese, and Lazaridi from Macedonia.

Nearly a dozen brands of beer are produced in Greece, as well as imports. Foreign brands made under licence include Amstel, Kaiser and Heineken; local labels are Fix (reckoned the best), Alfa, Mythos, Pils Hellas and Vergina. Corfu has its very own microbrewery near Arílas (www.corfubeer.com); its products, though expensive, are worth trying and include Royal Ionian pilsener and two ales.

Anise-flavoured *oúzo* is taken as an aperitif with ice and water; a compound in the anise flavouring makes the mix turn harmlessly cloudy. The most popular brands (like Mini and Plomari) come from Lésvos island. *Tsípouro* is a north-mainland variant of this grape-mash distillate, usually without anise, and popular on Corfu.

The local speciality liqueur is *koum kouat* (kumquat), a syrupy concoction produced from miniature citrus fruits grown here far from their native southeast Asia. For a diges-tif, Metaxa is the most popular domestic brandy, sold (in ascending order of strength and aging) in 3-, 5- and 7-star grades. Mavrodaphne is a fortified red dessert wine similar to Marsala.

Non-Alcoholic Drinks

Hot coffee (*kafés*) is typically *ellínikós* (generic Middle Eastern style, renamed 'Greek' from 'Turkish' in a fit of patriotism after the various Cyprus crises), freshly brewed in copper pots and served in small cups. It will probably arrive *glykós* (very sweet) unless you order *métrios* (medium) or *skétos* (without sugar); it's always accompanied by a glass of chilled water. Don't drink to the bottom as that's where the grounds settle.

Instant coffee is generically known as *nes* or *néskafe*, irrespective of brand; it's pretty unpalatable, an extra-strength formula for Mediterranean. There has been a recent backlash against it, so in large resorts and Kérkyra Town you can easily find proper brewed coffee (*gallikós* or *fíltro*), as well as competently executed cappuccino and espresso. *Fredduccino* – cold cappuccino – is also increasingly popular. Any milky coffee (though never with *ellínikós*) is *me gála*.

Frappés, cold instant coffee whipped up in a blender with sugar and milk is quite a fashionable drink. The milky version looks a little like a small Guinness and tastes like a coffee milkshake, but it's surprisingly refreshing in hot weather.

Soft drinks come in all the international varieties, while juices are most likely out of cardboard cartons. Bottled (*enfialoméno*) still mineral water is typically from Crete or the Greek mainland mountains. Souroti and Epsa are the most common domestic sparkling brands. Soda water is usually Tuborg.

Ginger Beer

Kérkyra Town (and Paxí) are the only places in Greece where you can get genuine 19th-century-style ginger beer, a delightful relic of British colonial rule. Locally called *tsitsibýra* (pronounced 'tsi-tsi-BEE-ra'), it should be served well chilled and is extremely refreshing in hot weather.

TO HELP YOU ORDER...

Could we have a table?	**Boroúme na éhoume éna trapézi?**
May we order, please?	**Na parangiloúme, parakaló?**
Bon appétit	**Kalí órexi**
I'm a vegetarian	**Íme hortofágos**
The bill, please	**To logariazmó, parakaló**
Cheers (as a toast)	**Yiámas**
A litre/a half litre	**Éna kiló/misó kilo**
Enjoy the next course too (literally, 'Good continuation')	**Kalí synnéhia**

plate	**piáto**	butter	**voútyro**
napkin	**hartopetséta**	sugar	**záhari**
cutlery	**maheropírouna**	salt	**aláti**
glass	**potíri**	pepper	**pipéri**
bread	**psomí**	oil	**ládi**

...AND READ THE MENU

fried	**tiganitó**	rabbit	**kounélli**
baked	**sto foúrno**	salad	**saláta**
roasted	**psitó**	tomatoes	**domátes**
grilled	**sta kárvouna**	olives	**eliés**
stuffed	**gemistá**	boiled greens	**hórta**
fish	**psári**		
small shrimp	**garídes**	runner/ string beans	**fasolákia**
octopus	**okhtapódi**		
red mullet	**barboúni**	aubergine/ eggplant	**melitzána**
swordfish	**xifías**		
meat	**kréas**	chickpeas	**revýthia**
meatballs	**keftedákia**	cheese	**tyrí**
beef, veal	**moskhári**	wine	**krasí**
pork	**hirinó**	beer	**býra**
chicken	**kotópoulo**	(chilled) water	**(pagoméno) neró**
lamb	**arní**		

PLACES TO EAT

Most restaurants outside of Kérkyra Town close between late October and late April inclusive; we've indicated exceptions, as well as cases where reservations are particularly advisable. All restaurant interiors are non-smoking by law (though some surreptitiously provide ash-trays on demand); if you wish to smoke overtly, this must usually be done outside. The following price ranges reflect the average cost of a two-course meal (per person) and a beer or share of bottled wine. These costs include VAT (sales tax), currently 23 percent, and notional service charge.

€€€€ over 40 euros   €€€ 30–40 euros

€€ 20–30 euros   € under 20 euros

KERKYRA TOWN

Akamatra Zythopoleio €–€€ *Prosaléndou 8–10, Spiliá district, tel: 26610 40101.* Open Mon–Sat, noon–3.30pm & 7.30–11pm. At this welcoming, compact spot with original medieval arches and pointed brick walls, inexpensive lunch specials include bean soup, cannelloni and giouvarláki (rissole soup), though dinner fare falls in the higher price category. As the name indicates, they're strong on beer, both imported and the local, light-flavoured red beer and ale brewed at Corfu's own microbrewery in Arílas. Cash only.

Aroma Thessalonikis € *Agíou Vasilíou 13, Kérkyra Town, tel: 26610 80370.* Open daily, early until late. The only sit-down spot for desserts in the old town, whose stock in trade is Salonika specialities like kazandibí pudding and trígona pastries. Cash only.

Art Gallery Café € *Gardens off east wing of Palace of St Michael and St George.* Open daily 9am–8pm. Tucked away on a quiet terrace by the Municipal Art Gallery, this is the perfect spot to rest while sightseeing or as a prelude to an evening out. In some seasons the admission ticket to the gallery includes a coffee and small cake. Drinks and snacks only. Cash only.

La Cucina €€ *Guilford 15, tel: 26610 45029*. Open daily 7pm–midnight March–Nov, weekend nights only Dec–Feb. Fight for a table outside at this competent Italian eatery, which does excellent pizzas and handmade pasta dishes. Success has prompted the opening of a more contemporary-decor annexe at the corner of Moustóxydou and Guilford, 50 paces away, which is used exclusively during the cooler months.

La Famiglia €€ *Maniarízi & Arlióti 16 (Kandoúni Bízi), alley between Filellínon and Nikifórou Theotóki, tel: 26610 30270*. Open 8pm–12.30am Mon–Sat, open Sun in August, closed Sun/Mon winter. Efficiently run Greek/Italian bistro specialising in salads, pasta dishes like *linguini al cozze*, a few token Greek platters such as leek pie, and Italian desserts. Excellent bulk wine from the Neméa region or Santoríni. Limited seating, so reservations always essential.

Khrysi (O Ninos) € *Sevastianoú 44*. Open daily noon–late. A classic budget feed in Kérkyra Town: assorted traditional estiatório casserole dishes, plus good take-away gýros and souvláki. Limited sidewalk tables and a stuffy interior make this a better bet for the off-season. Cash only.

Khryssomallis (Babis) € *Nikifórou Theotókou 6, tel: 26610 30342*. Open daily noon–10.30pm. The sign says *zythopsitopolío* ('beer-hall-grill'), but it's actually the last traditional oven-food place in the Old Town: stews, *hórta*, *moussakás*, stuffed cabbage leaves, lentil soup and so forth, accompanied by smooth but potent red wine. From the outside tables on the street you can just see the Listón. The Durrells ate here during their 1930s stay; the restaurant has been around even longer. Cash only.

Mouragia €€ *Arseníou 15, Mourágia quay, tel: 26610 33815*. Open Apr–Nov noon–12.30am. A good mix of seafood such as flash-fried *atherína* (sand smelt) and Corfiot specialities such as *sofríto* and *pastitsáda*, plus competent starters at this seaside ouzerí – though views to the sea, and Vídos islet, are over the road. Cash only.

Rouvas € *Stamatíou Desýlla 13, tel: 26610 31182*. Mon–Sat 9am–6pm, all year. A classic lunchtime hangout that – despite an unglamorous location in the Pórto Reále bazaar area – attracts visiting celebrity chefs like Rick Stein to see just how traditional island cooking should be. Recipes – sometimes on the oily side – include *pastítsio*, artichokes with peas, meat stews, fish soup and hearty salads. Unlike many such places, it has a cheery, appealing interior often still crowded at 4pm. Cash only.

Rex €€–€€€ *Kapodistríou 66, tel: 26610 39649.* Open all day daily. Established in 1932, the Rex is something of a Kérkyra Town institution. Signature dishes include fish soup (in winter), orange-fleshed squash turnover, portobello mushrooms with cheese and other generic Mediterranean recipes. Tables outdoors, or inside (dress up a bit for the latter).

Theotoki Brothers (Kerkyraïki Paradosiaki Taverna) €€ *Alkiviádi Dári 69, Anemómylos, tel: 26610 48161.* Open Apr–Oct daily noon–4.30pm and 7–11.30pm. The best of several tavernas with tables out in the eucalyptus park here. A full range of dishes like *tsigarélli* (greens stir-fried with chilli), grills, plus some seafood (often frozen), issue from an incredibly narrow kitchen.

Tsipouradiko € *Prosaléndou 8–10, behind the Efetío (Appeals Court), Spiliá, tel: 26610 82240.* Open Mon–Sat 8pm–1am. Tsípouro is the distilled grape-mash spirit popular on the mainland (but also many islands), accompanied here by such platters as grilled mushrooms, courgette pie, *tiganiá* (pork stir-fry), little fishes, and aubergine specialities. There is also decent bulk wine. The place is always packed with students and the bohemian set thanks to the warm atmosphere and friendly prices. Smoking allowed in the upstairs loft, or outside in the summer courtyard. Large groups must reserve, or be prepared for a long wait. Cash only.

Venetian Well €€€–€€€€ *Platía Kremastí, northeast of Orthodox Cathedral, Campiello district, tel: 26610 44761.* Open Apr–Oct daily lunch and dinner, otherwise Thur–Sat dinner only. Tucked away through an arch, with summertime tables set around the eponymous well, is some of the town's most expensive global fusion cuisine – 'transnational dishes' as the management puts it. Recipes change seasonally, but in the past have included duck in plum sauce or dolmádes with wild rice. The interior features murals imitating tiles or incorporating inscriptions, mismatched furniture and an ethno-trance soundtrack. Excellent (and pricey) wine list. Cash only.

THE SOUTH

Alonaki Bay €–€€ *Paralía Alonáki, near Korissíon Lagoon and Gardíki Castle, tel: 26610 75872.* Open daily Apr–Oct lunch and dinner. Good country recipes, strong on vegetables and seafood at shady tables on a terrace overlooking the sea. Their version of *biánko*, with *kéfalos* (grey mullet) hygienically raised in the lake and garnished with marsh samphire (*Salicornia europaea*), is to die for. Locals, and free-range chickens underfoot, usually outnumber tourists here – one of the best endorsements. If you can't tear yourself away from this lovely spot, they have inexpensive rooms to rent upstairs as well. Cash only.

Boukari Beach €€ *Boúkari, 4km (2.5 miles) beyond Mesongí, 600m before the jetty, tel: 26620 51791, www.boukaribeach.gr.* Open lunch and dinner, Easter–Oct. The best of the seafood tavernas at this seashore hamlet, in an idyllic setting with spectacular views up Corfu's east coast. Typical offerings might include mussels as a starter, heaping salads, succulent octopus and a range of patently fresh scaly fish at fair prices. The Vlahopoulos family are accomplished hosts, and also have accommodation *(see page 137)*.

Klimataria tou Bellou €–€€ *main village square, Benítses, tel: 26610 71201, www.klimataria-restaurant.gr.* Open Mon–Sat dinner only, Sunday lunch; winter weekends only; but closed 1 Dec–15 Jan. Cult seafood taverna known for purveying only fresh items, and for assiduous service from father-and-son team Nikos and Kostas. Fish is sold by portion or by weight, and includes some innovative dishes like sardine *bourdéto*; starters such as leek salad and steamed mussels are commendable too. Good Neméa bulk white wine. Blink and you'll miss the mere eight tables outside, so reservations are highly advisable.

Trypas €€€ *Kynopiástes, 7km (4.5 miles) southwest of Kérkyra, tel: 26610 56333.* Open daily May–Oct supper only; otherwise Fri/

Sat night only until 11pm. Classic if rather touristy taverna where the set-price table d'hôte menu allows a fair sampling of Corfiot dishes (*pastitsáda*, sausage, *stifádo*, *sofríto*) along with some inappropriate dishes like shrimp cocktail, accompanied by very good house red and white wine. The small winter dining room, originally opened as a grocery shop in 1936, is dominated by old bottles, gourds and photos of past celebrity clients. During summer, there's folk dancing out by the courtyard seating.

NORTH OF KERKYRA TOWN

Etrusco €€€€ *Káto Korakiána village, on the road down to Dassiá, tel: 26610 93342, www.etrusco.gr.* Open Apr–Oct, supper only. Top-calibre nouvelle Italian cooking by father, son and spouses, served in a carefully restored country manor. Specialities like pappardelle with duck and truffles, octopus carpaccio, lamb baked with garlic and kumquat sauce and a 200-label wine list don't come cheap, but this has been ranked as one of the best five Greek tavernas outside of Athens. Advance reservations required.

Roula's €€ *Kondókali, well-signposted on the Nisí Gerékou peninsula; tel: 26610 91832.* Summer daily lunch and dinner, winter dinner Mon–Sat, Sun lunch. A favourite venue for a seafood meal, especially out on the terrace overlooking the marina. Scaly fish like sykiós (corb) is well priced and grilled to perfection; ask for it to be butterflied (petáli style). Starter portions are decent, though opt for beer or ouzo rather than their rather average bulk wine.

THE NORTHEAST

Cavo Barbaro (Fotis) €€ *Avláki beach, east of Kassiópi, tel: 26630 81905.* Open daily all day May–Oct. A competent beach taverna, with welcoming service. A few *magirevtá* dishes like risotto and *soutzoukákia* at lunch; more grills after dark, plus homemade *glyká koutalioú* (candied fruit). There's seating on the lawn, or on flagstones under a pergola, and plenty of parking. The only thing 'barbarous' here can be the wind, as there's no shelter; check direction and strength before heading downhill. Cash only.

Fagopotion €€–€€€ *Ágios Stéfanos Sinión; tel: 26630 82020.* Open daily for lunch and dinner Easter–Oct, Fri–Sat dinner and Sun lunch otherwise. The most accomplished of the several waterside tavernas here, Fagopotion only opened in 2008 but has already established an enviable reputation for its traditional recipes, fresh (not farmed) fish caught around the Diapóndia islets and fair prices given the posh location. Signature dishes include roast lamb, rabbit stew, chard-based tsigarélli and melt-in-the-mouth octopus (it's blanched prior to grilling). Kosta's rosé bulk wine is interesting.

Kalami Beach €€–€€€ *Kalámi beach, tel: 26630 91168, www. kalamibeach.com.* Open daily lunch/dinner May–Oct. The USPs at this restaurant can be summed up as a prime beachside location, willing service and normal prices for scaly fish (brought in on the family's own boat). Other items are on the pricey side, including the lobsters awaiting their doom in the aquarium tanks which form part of the decor.

Kouloura €€–€€€ *Kouloúra cove, tel: 26630 91253.* Open daily all day Apr–Oct, though last orders are rather early at 9.30pm. For 'Kensington-on-Sea,' moderately priced seafood, a large selection of *mezédes*, plus unusually elaborate *píttes* (baked pies) and pulse dishes at this impeccably set taverna overlooking one of Corfu's most photogenic anchorages. Reservations needed in peak season. Cash only.

Little Italy €€ *Kassiopí, opposite Grivas supermarket, tel: 26630 81749.* Open summer daily for dinner, winter Wed–Sat only. Jolly trattoria in an old stone house run by Italian brothers. The fare includes salmon in pastry parcels, pizza, pastas smothered in freshly made sauces. *Limoncello digestif* on the house. Cash only.

Nikolas €–€€ *Agní cove south end, tel: 26630 91243, www.agnibay. com.* Open daily May–Oct lunch and dinner; may open winter weekends. This taverna is the oldest one here, built as a family home and café in 1892. Today, Perikles and his family serve Corfiot specialities like aubergine-and-cheese bourékia and lamb kapamá, along with their own wines (the bulk red is excellent).

Service usually copes well with typical crowds. Tear yourself away from the picturesque view to browse the old photos and maps lining the walls inside.

Toula €€€ *Agní cove, tel: 26630 91350*. Open daily lunch and supper May–Oct. Worth a special mention for its professional demeanour, nice line in hot mezédes and the house special *garídes Toula* – grilled prawns with spicy mixed-rice pilaff. Any of the seafood main dishes, washed down by excellent bulk white wine, is a likely winner here.

THE NORTH AND NORTHWEST

Akrogiali €–€€ *Far south end of the bay, Ágios Geórgios Págon, tel: 6977 334278*. Open daily 15 May–6 Oct. A bumpy, wash-out-prone track leads 1,500m (1,640yds) south from the beach to this little eyrie (marked by a windmill). Per-kilo fish prices are quite low for Corfu, and there are appealing oddities like carrot salad and fish croquettes as *mezédes*. The lowest seating terrace is lapped by the sea.

Foros € *Paleá Períthia, tel:6955 950459*. Open daily May–Oct, weekends only otherwise. One of the first tavernas in this once-deserted Venetian village, working out of a former café on the original square, and still one of the best – Rick Stein has called in approvingly. The emphasis here is on grills, but you can have a very enjoyable *mezédes*-only meal – sausages, *kremydópita* (onion turnover), stuffed peppers – while downing *tsípouro* or bulk wine. Save room for their famous *karydópita* (walnut cake) with ice cream. Cash only.

Kohili €€ *Ágios Stéfanos Gýrou, tel: 26630 51629*. Open dinner only, May–Oct. For a romantic evening, book a table amidst wicker chairs and gauzy curtains at this gourmet restaurant in the Delfino Blu Hotel. From the veranda tables you'll have a stupendous view across the ocean into the sunset. The fare is generic Mediterranean, encompassing risottos, pasta, salads and some Greek platters, complemented by fine local wines, including some of the restaurant's own production.

Xenykhtis (The Night Owl) € *northerly approach to Afiónas village, above Ágios Geórgios Págon, tel: 26630 51314.* Open daily except Sun lunch May–Oct; otherwise Fri–Sat evenings. Friendly, tiny, somewhat ramshackle grill-taverna named after the local nocturnal avians. Every imaginable charcoal-grilled meat served up by returned New York Corfiot Nick and his wife Linda. Cash only.

THE WEST

Antonis € *Pélekas, tel: 26610-94289.* Open daily lunch and dinner much of the year. The best value of several tavernas here, with a good line in grills, *mezédes* and salads. They also have the calmest outdoor terrace in what can be a rather traffic-plagued village. Cash only.

Elizabeth's € *Doukádes village centre, tel: 26610 94284.* Open daily lunch and dinner most of the year. Elizabeth's has been going since the 1940s, and is now mostly in the hands of grand-daughter Elizabeth. Signature dishes include cockerel pastitsáda with extra-fat noodles, and wholesome peas with potatoes. The purplish bulk wine is rough and ready, as is the *objet trouvé* decor (ancient bottles and a jukebox which sadly has expired). For once, a place that's definitely more fun to eat at inside than out. Cash only.

PAXI

La Rosa di Paxos €€–€€€ *Lákka port quay, tel: 26620 31471.* Open for lunch and supper, May–Oct. The Greco-Italian management is reflected in the blend of flavours for scaly fish, pasta (including seafood linguini) and other generic Mediterranean dishes. The place for a last-night treat.

Vassilis (Kostakis) €€€ *Longós quay, tel: 26620 31587.* Open for lunch and supper, May–Oct. Now often known by its alias after the son who's taken it over, this has grown from a grilled-fish specialist to an all-round restaurant with proper table nappery and imaginative recipes like stuffed mushrooms and peppers, baked-meat dishes or various oven pies.

A–Z TRAVEL TIPS

A Summary of Practical Information

A

ACCOMMODATION

Many hotels are heavily booked with package tours in summer, especially during the first three weeks of August, so advance reservations are strongly recommended. If you do arrive without one, travel agencies in the resorts or Kérkyra Town may know of available accommodation.

Hotels are rated from 1-star to 5-star, based more on their common areas and amenities than the actual rooms. Prices can vary widely within each category, while luxury (5-star) establishments are not price-controlled. Thus, a 3-star hotel room may be just as comfortable as a 5-star room, but common areas will not include a conference room, hairdresser, swimming pool or multiple restaurants. All hotels of 2-star rating and above are en suite, clean and reasonably furnished, and should provide breakfast.

Villas and Apartments. Corfu has more villas, multi-bedroom apartments and studios than many other Greek tourist centres. Accommodation ranges from simple flats to lavishly appointed summer homes – often tastefully converted from a traditional house or houses – complete with swimming pool. In the UK, several companies specialise in secluded luxury villas on both Corfu and Paxí: CV Travel (www.cvtravel.co.uk), Sunvil (www.sunvil.co.uk), Greek Islands Club (www.gicthevillacollection.com), Simpson Travel (www.simpsontravel.com) and Travel à la Carte (www.travelalacarte.co.uk). More affordable are Meon Villas (www.meonvillas.co.uk), Direct Holidays (www.directholidays.co.uk), Thomson Villas with Pools (www.thomson.co.uk) and Simply Travel (www.simplytravel.co.uk).

I'd like a single/double room	**Tha íthela éna monóklino/díklino**
How much do you charge?	**Póso hreónete?**

AIRPORT

Located 2km (1.2 miles) from the capital, Corfu's lagoon-side airport (CFU) is capable of handling all but the largest jets. However, time spent here can sometimes be frustrating, with long waits for baggage and other inconveniences.

Here are some useful tips for surviving potential pre-departure pandemonium at the airport. Take your own food and drink with you, as delays are common and the refreshment outlets available may not be able to cope with large backlogs of passengers awaiting their flights. Facilities and seating in the airside lounge are inadequate, so the best place to find a space to sit down – unfortunately, often on the floor – is at the far end of the Arrivals hall. In case of really long, confirmed delays, it's better to walk the 700m/yds to the shore of Garítsa Bay where proper cafés and tavernas await.

The terminal building has several car hire desks and (inadequate) refreshment stands. The currency-exchange office opens from 9am until 2am if there are international flights scheduled to land late at night. (It's a good idea to arrive with a few euros in hand, in case the airport office is closed, though there is at least one ATM in the airport.)

There is no bus service linking the airport with Kérkyra Town. Taxis charge a set, inflated €10 for the short run into town. Prebooked car rental is so advantageously priced that there's little point in submitting to their tender mercies.

You can track flight arrivals and departures at www.europe-airports.com/greece.

B

BICYCLE AND SCOOTER HIRE

You can hire bicycles and scooters in all the tourist centres. However, many package operators warn clients against scooters for legitimate fear of an accident (and to drum up more business for organised excursions). It is vital that you check that scooter/motorbike use does not invalidate your holiday insurance.

Usually, to hire a motorbike with an engine larger than 50 cc you must be at least 18 years old and hold a Class A1 (light motorcycle) licence. However, since 2011 Greek law has included 50cc bikes under the A1 category, and the old dodge of using a car driving, or Class P, license will probably not suffice – zealous police are fining both renting agencies and riders up to €1,000 for violations. It is also illegal to ride without a crash helmet – the fines issued at checkpoints are similarly draconian.

It is certainly not advisable to ride a motorbike in a swimsuit, since burns or scrapes resulting from even a slight accident could be appalling. Inspect brakes and tyres before hiring, and drive with care. Even on good roads there are occasional potholes or treacherous gravel patches.

Bicycle hire is less common because of Corfu's mountainous terrain, but a good place for serious bikers is the Corfu Mountain Bike Shop (tel: 26610 93344; www.mountainbikecorfu.gr), on the main road at Dassiá. It offers top-quality bikes and can also organise expeditions. You can also try Mountain Mania in Sidári (tel: 26630 95975, www.mountainmaniacorfu.com).

BUDGETING FOR YOUR TRIP

Corfu is not the cheapest of the Greek islands, and probably as costly as most other Mediterranean destinations. In high season, the rate for a good 4-star hotel is around €140 minimum per night for a double room. Booking an airfare/accommodation package will yield a substantial saving.

A three-course meal plus drinks in a decent restaurant or taverna costs around €20–30 per person. Car hire ranges from about €15 per day (low season) to €25 per day in peak season, if pre-booked online. Public transport and museum fees are inexpensive.

C

CAR HIRE

It is definitely worth hiring a car in order to explore Corfu. As elsewhere in Greece, this is not particularly cheap in peak season, but it is certainly less expensive than touring by taxi, and less frustrating than coping with irregular public transport. For a decent family-sized car in high season, budget €250 minimum per week, and choose a model with air conditioning.

In high season, advance on-line reservation is essential. Some of the best consolidator websites include www.skycars.co.uk, www.auto-europe.co.uk/com, www.carrentals.co.uk, and www.rentalcargroup.com.

Those intending to hire a car should carry an International Driving Permit if from the US, Canada or Australia (national licences alone are not valid, and there are heavy fines if you're detected driving without an IDP). Alternatively all European Economic Area national driver's licences are accepted, provided that they have been held for one full year and the driver is over 21 years of age (sometimes 23 years for certain agencies). You will also need a credit or debit card for a deposit.

Many brochure rates seem attractive because they do not include personal insurance, collision damage waiver (CDW) or VAT at 23 percent. Most agencies have a waiver excess of between €400 and €600 – the amount you're responsible for if your vehicle gets smashed or stolen, even with CDW coverage. It is strongly suggested you purchase extra cover (often called Super CDW or Liability Waiver Surcharge) to reduce this risk to zero;

I'd like to hire a car (tomorrow)	**Tha íthela na nikiáso éna avtokínito (ávrio)**
What's the hire charge per day?	**Póso kostízi tin iméra?**

UK or North American residents can buy good-value annual policies from entities like Insurance4CarHire (www.insurance4 carhire.com).

CLIMATE

July and August are the sunniest, hottest and busiest tourist months. You may prefer to stay between mid-May and late June or from early September to mid-October. At any time outside June to August it might rain. Corfu is, after all, one of the greenest Greek islands.

In winter it rains very hard. November through February are the wettest months and January the coldest, but even during mid-winter, frost is rare except at altitude. Spring, when Corfu bursts with wild flowers, is the best time for walking.

The chart shows each month's average air and sea temperature in Celsius and Fahrenheit, and the average number of hours of sunshine per day.

		J	F	M	A	M	J	J	A	S	O	N	D
Air	°C	10	10	12	15	19	24	27	26	23	19	15	12
Air	°F	50	50	54	59	66	75	81	79	73	66	59	54
Sea	°C	15	15	15	16	18	21	24	25	24	21	19	18
Sea	°F	59	59	59	61	64	70	75	77	75	70	66	64
Sunshine hours			5	6	7	7	9	10	11	12	9	6	4	3

CLOTHING

Clothing is almost always casual on Corfu. However, it is appropriate to dress up a little for a night in Kérkyra Town. Choose lightweight cotton clothes in spring and summer, and a warm jacket, sweater and rainwear in autumn or winter. A pocket umbrella is a good idea at any season except mid-summer.

CRIME AND SAFETY (see also Emergencies and Police)

The Corfiots, like most Greeks, are scrupulously honest. However, of late organised burglary rings are targeting foreign-owned or tenanted villas in the north of the island, so take appropriate precautions. Those staying in a hotel should use the room safe rather than circulate with excess valuables. Car break-ins (especially at isolated beach parking areas) are not unknown. Take a photocopy of your passport, rather than the original, out with you (you're required to have official ID on your person at all times in Greece).

Possession of recreational drugs is a serious matter in Greece. Keep prescription drugs in their original containers, and keep documentation handy for insulin syringes.

D

DRIVING

Road Conditions. Main roads are generally very good, but secondary roads are some of the narrowest and most treacherous on any of the Greek islands. Curves are often indicated too late, sometimes unsignposted and never banked correctly. If there is a mirror on a bend, brake and downshift – it is probably going to be extremely tight or narrow, or perhaps both. Rockslides are common in the rainy season, and broken shoulders or potholes are not unknown on even the best-paved stretches; anything marked 'unsurfaced' on a map can be very rough indeed. Drive with extreme caution, as you are responsible for damage sustained to the underside of your hire car, even with comprehensive coverage.

Rules and Regulations. Drive on the right side and pass on the left. Roundabouts and traffic lights are eccentrically arranged by north-European standards. If an oncoming driver flashes the lights, it means 'Stay where you are, I'm coming through', not 'Go ahead'. Seat belts are obligatory as is the carrying of your driving licence while at the wheel. Speed limits are 50kph (30mph) inside built-up

Are we on the right road for…?	**Páme kalá gia…?**
Fill the tank please, with (unleaded) petrol	**Parakaló, goméste to reservoír (me amólyvdi)**
My car has broken down	**To avtokinitó mou éhi halási**
There's been an accident	**Éhi gínei distýhima**

areas, 80kph (50mph). In practice, however, Corfu's winding roads usually set the speed limit – it's difficult to safely exceed 50kph (30mph).

Fuel. Unless you are on the top of Mt Pandokrátor, you will never be far from a filling station. However, in rural areas they are open only until about 8pm and closed on Sunday. On busy main roads and in resorts they open daily from early until late. A few big filling stations have after-hours automatic-sales pumps, using euro notes.

If You Need Help. Your car hire office should provide contact numbers for breakdown service. If you are involved in an accident with another vehicle and/or with significant personal in-

Detour	**ΠΑΡΑΚΑΨΗ/Parákampsi**
Parking	**ΠΑΡΚΙΓΚ/Párking**
Forbidden	**…ΑΠΑΓΟΡΕΥΕΤΑΙ/ …apagorévete**
Be careful	**ΠΡΟΣΟΧΗ/Prosohí**
Bus stop	**ΣΤΑΣΗ ΛΕΟΦΟΡΙΟΥ/Stasí leoforíou**
Stop	**ΣΤΑΜΑΤΑ/Stamáta**
For pedestrians	**ΓΙΑ ΠΕΖΟΥΣ/Gia pezoús**
Danger	**ΚΙΝΔΙΝΟΣ/Kíndinos**
No entry	**ΑΠΑΓΟΡΕΥΕΤΑΙ Η ΕΙΣΟΔΟΣ/ Apagorévete i ísodos**

Embassies and Consulates 121

Corfu roads readily generate punctures – unfortunately, tyre-repair shops are concentrated in the middle of the island, around Gouviá. A good one there is Pangratis, on the northeast side of the highway (tel: 26610 91495).

Road Signs. On main roads these are in Greek and Latin (Western) letters; on secondary roads they may just be in Greek. Critical junctions are atrociously indicated, with vital signs either uprooted or hidden by foliage.

E

ELECTRICITY

Corfu has 220-volt/50-cycle AC current. Sockets are two-pin, so bring an adapter or transformer with you as necessary.

EMBASSIES AND CONSULATES

There are United Kingdom and Republic of Ireland consular offices in Kérkyra Town. Embassies of main countries are located in Athens.

Australian Embassy and Consulate: Level 6, Thon Building, junction Kifisías & Alexándras, 115 21 Athens; tel: 210 87 04 000, www.greece.embassy.australia.gov.au

British Vice Consulate: Mantzárou 18, Kérkyra Town; tel: 26610 23457.

British Embassy: Ploutárhou 1, 106 75 Athens; tel: 210 72 72 600, http://ukingreece.fco.gov.uk/en

Canadian Embassy: Gennadíou 4, 115 21 Athens; tel: 210 72 73 400.

Irish Honorary Consulate: 20A Kapodistríou Street, Kérkyra Town; tel: 26610 33411.

Irish Embassy: Vassiléos Konstandínou 7, 106 74 Athens; tel: 210 72 32 771.

South African Embassy and Consulate: Kifisías 60, 151 25 Marousi, Athens; tel: 210 61 06 645.

US Embassy and Consulate: Vassilísis Sofías 91, 101 60 Athens; tel: 210 72 12 951; http://athens.usembassy.gov

EMERGENCIES

Police, tel: **100**.
Ambulance, tel: **166**.
Fire, tel: **199**.

Fire!	**Fotiá!**
Help!	**Voíthia!**
Police!	**Astynomía!**
Stop!	**Stamatíste!**

G

GAY AND LESBIAN TRAVELLERS

Corfu has no specific gay scene but attitudes in the resorts are generally relaxed. Be discreet in the conservative rural communities. Homosexual practice is legal in Greece for people aged over 17 years old.

GETTING THERE

It is possible to cross Europe overland and take a ferry from Venice, Ancona, Brindisi or Bari in Italy to Corfu. But for most visitors, air travel (around 3 hours' flight time from Britain) is the only practical route. Charter flights from the UK link a dozen British airports to Corfu; Jet2, easyJet, Thomsonfly, Monarch, Thomas Cook and Ryanair provide seasonal scheduled services from several UK airports. If you are travelling from North America, you might find it just as economical to fly to London and pick up a cheap flight from there.

H

HEALTH AND MEDICAL CARE

Doctors and dentists are concentrated in Kérkyra Town; your hotel or apartment owner will be able to find you one who speaks English. Most resorts have a public medical clinic.

The capital's hospital and general clinic operate a 24-hour emergency service that dispatches ambulances to any point on the island with admirable speed. The new, 2010-opened Corfu General Hospital is 4km (2 miles) out of Kérkyra Town, in Kondókali. Corfu General Clinic is located on the main Paleokastrítsa road, just outside Kérkyra Town centre (tel: 26610 36044 or 26610 22946). Emergency treatment is given free, although this only covers immediate needs. EU residents can get further free treatment with a European Health Insurance Card (EHIC; www.ehic.org.uk). It is advisable to take out additional travel insurance to cover you for protracted treatment or repatriation.

A green cross on a white background identifies a chemist (pharmacy) – *farmakío* (**ΦΑΡΜΑΚΕΙΟ**). They are normally open only 9am–2pm Monday to Friday, but a notice on the door specifies the nearest one for after-hours/weekend service.

a doctor/dentist	**énas giatrós/odontogiatrós**
hospital	**nosokomío**
an upset stomach	**anakatoméno stomáhi**
sunstroke	**ilíasi**
a fever	**pyretós**

L

LANGUAGE

Only in remote countryside spots will non-Greek-speaking tourists run into serious communication problems. You will find that basic

English is spoken almost everywhere, as are Italian, German and French, to some degree. Both the *Berlitz Greek Phrase Book & CD*, or *Earworms Rapid Greek* volumes cover nearly all situations you are likely to encounter.

Stress is a very important feature of the Greek language, denoted by an accent above the vowel of the syllable to be emphasised. We

A	α	a	as in *fa*ther
B	β	v	as in veto
Γ	γ	g	as in *g*o (except before *i* and e sounds, when it's like the *y* in *y*es)
Δ	δ	d	sounds like *th* in *th*en
E	ε	e	as in *g*et
Z	ζ	z	same as in English
H	η	i	as in *ski*
Θ	θ	th	as in *th*in
I	ι	i	as in *ski*
K	κ	k	same as in English
Λ	λ	l	same as in English
M	μ	m	same as in English
N	ν	n	same as in English
Ξ	ξ	x	as in *box*
O	ο	o	as in *road*
Π	π	p	same as in English
P	ρ	r	same as in English
Σ	σ, ς	s	as in *ki*s*s*, except like *z* before *m* or *g* sounds
T	τ	t	same as in English
Y	υ	y	as in *country*
Φ	φ	f	same as in English
X	χ	h	rough, as in Scottish *lo*c*h*

Ψ	ψ	ps	as in *tipsy*
Ω	ω	o	as in *long*
AI	αι	e	as in *hay*
AY	αυ	av	as in *avant-garde*
EI	ει	i	as in *ski*
EY	ευ	ev	as in *ever*
OI	οι	i	as in *ski*
OY	ου	ou	as in *soup*
ΓΓ	γγ	ng	as in *longer*
ΓΚ	γκ	g	as in *gone*
ΓΞ	γξ	nx	as in *anxious*
ΜΠ	μπ	b or mb	as in *beg* or *compass*
ΝΤ	ντ	d or nd	as in *dog* or *under*

have indicated proper stress in all of our transliterations of multisyllable words.

The table *above* lists the Greek letters in their upper- and lower-case forms, followed by the closest individual or combined letters to which they correspond in the English language, and a pronunciation guide. Do not be alarmed if you encounter other transliterations on Corfu – several schemes exist. For example, the word *ágios* is often also spelled *ághios* and *áyios* in the Roman alphabet, although it is always pronounced the same.

M

MAPS

The folding Kérkyra Town plan handed out by the tourist-info kiosk on Platía Sarókko is the best available. For a commercial touring map of the entire island, plump for either the 1:60,000 Road Editions product or the 1:90,000 Emvelia title – bought before arrival.

MEDIA

Newspapers: In season, major English newspapers can be bought in resorts one day after publication. Some English tabloids have European editions printed in Greece and available the same day. The daily *E-Kathimerini* (www.ekathimerini.com) included inside the *International Herald Tribune* is also available, as is the English-language *Athens News* (www.athensnews.gr), published each Friday in print form.

Television: Most large hotels have satellite TV services, which include news channels such as CNN and BBC World. On Greek stations American and English films and other imported programmes are broadcast in the original language, with Greek subtitles.

MONEY

Currency: For the time being, the euro (€) is used in Greece. Notes are denominated in 5, 10, 20, 50, 100, 200 and 500 euros; coins in 1 and 2 euros and 1, 2, 5, 10, 20 and 50 cents, known as *leptá* in Greece. Notes of 100 euros and above are regarded with suspicion, as counterfeit, and can often only be broken down in banks.

Currency exchange: Most banks exchange foreign currency but charge a commission (usually 1–3 percent) for the service. Exchange rates appear on a digital display, and are identical for each bank.

You can also change money at a bureaux de change inside travel agencies, open longer hours than banks. Some advertise commission-free transactions, but exchange rates are often inferior to those of banks.

I want to change some pounds/dollars	**Thélo na alláxo merikés líres/meriká dollária**
Can I pay with this credit card?	**Boró na pliróso me aftí tin pistotikí kárta?**

ATMs: There are cash machines in every Corfiot town or resort of over a few hundred inhabitants. These are the most convenient way to get euros.

Credit cards: Many hotels, restaurants, travel agencies, filling stations and shops accept credit cards, but there is still a sizeable minority that do not, and out in the countryside credit cards are not generally accepted. Some companies charge extra for credit card purchases.

Travellers cheques: These are not recommended for use in Greece – expect severe delays or outright refusals in banks or exchange bureaux.

OPENING TIMES

Opening times vary between official organisations and privately owned shops and cafés, and also between high and low season. Almost everybody closes at mid-afternoon, and official entities will not reopen later; if you need to get anything official done, do so in the morning.

We give opening days and hours for museums and archaeological sites in the text, but remember that the last admission ticket is generally sold 20 minutes before closing time. Shops are open Monday, Wednesday and Saturday 9am–2.30pm, closing at 2pm on Tuesday, Thursday and Friday but open additionally 5.30–8.30pm. In peak season, they may stay open throughout the day until midnight, especially if selling tourist-related products. Supermarkets open 8.30am–9pm Mon–Fri, 8.30am–8pm Sat; a very few may work 10am–4pm Sunday. Restaurants and tavernas do lunch from just after noon until 3.30pm, and begin dinner service at around 6.30pm, but most Greek families don't eat until after 9pm. Most banks are open Mon–Thur 8am–2.30pm, Fri 8am–2pm.

P

POLICE (see Emergencies)

Regular police officers wear two-toned blue uniforms. Tourist police also wear blue uniforms displaying a small national flag indicating which language they speak other than Greek.

If you need to report an incident to the police, go to the police station closest to the scene of the crime. Each group of villages has a designated police station.

Traffic police check car documents and driving licences, operate speed traps and issue hefty fines for illegal parking. Car hire companies will use your credit-card details to pay ignored parking tickets; you have 10 working days to pay moving violations in person. Failing that, a court date will be set, and a summons sent to your home address. Failure to appear will result in an extra conviction for contempt of court, and make re-entry to Greece extremely awkward.

| Where's the nearest police station? | Pou íne to kondinótero astynomikó tmíma? |

POST OFFICES

Post offices have blue-and-yellow livery, and are marked 'Elliniká Takhydromía' in Greek plus 'Hellenic Post' in English, with a stylised Hermes head as the logo. Stamps can be bought here, or at postal agencies (usually small shops).

Post offices are generally open Mon–Fri 7.30am–2pm. The main Kérkyra Town post office at the corner of Alexándhras and Zafiropoúlou is open Mon–Fri 7.30am–8pm (until 2.30pm for money orders and parcels) and Saturday mornings during the months of July and August. Registered letters and parcels to non-EU destinations are checked before being sent, so don't seal them beforehand.

Mail boxes are yellow with the same Hermes-head logo, but in rural areas they are not emptied every day. Most hotels will post letters and postcards for you. Allow 4–7 days for postcards to Europe, 9–14 days for the rest of the world.

A stamp for this letter/ postcard	**Éna grammatósimo giavtó to grámma/ giavtí tin kart postál**

PUBLIC HOLIDAYS

Banks, offices and shops are closed on the following national holidays, as well as during some local festivals:

1 January	New Year's Day (*Protohroniá*)
6 January	Epiphany (*Theofánia*)
25 March	Greek Independence/Annunciation (*Evangelismós*) Day
1 May	May Day
15 August	Dormition of the Virgin (*Kímisis tis Panagías*)
28 October	National *Ohi* ('No') Day, celebrates 1940 defiance of Italians
25 December	Christmas (*Hristoúgena*)
26 December	*Sýnaxis tis Panagías* (Gathering of the Virgin's Entourage)

Moveable religious festivals:
The first day of Lent (*Katharí Deftéra*/Clean Monday), Good Friday, Easter Monday and *tou Agíou Pnévmatos*/Whit Monday.

R

RELIGION

Corfu, like the rest of Greece, is largely Greek Orthodox in faith. There is, however, a sizeable but well-integrated Catholic minority with a handful of functioning churches in Kérkyra Town. The Holy Trinity Anglican Church at Mavíli 21, in the Pórta Remoúnda district of Kérkyra Town, holds weekly services – visitors are welcome.

You must dress modestly to visit churches or monasteries, which normally means long trousers for men, a long skirt for women and covered shoulders for both sexes. Men might be allowed to wear long shorts, and wraps are sometimes provided for under-dressed women.

T

TELEPHONES

Since deregulation of the local telecoms market, a number of providers offer competition to the state-run OTE. OTE still, however, maintains most of the increasingly scarce public booths. Kiosks and newsagents sell OTE calling-cards in various unit denominations, as well as other products (including discount long-distance cards and local mobile top-up cards).

Most hotels of two stars and above have direct-dial lines out, but add a huge surcharge to the cost of calls. Avoid this by using a prepaid, 12-digit-code card with an access number.

Dialling from abroad, the country code for Greece is 30. Within Greece, all phone numbers have ten digits; fixed lines begin with 2, mobiles with 6. There are no longer any area codes as such in Greece – what were the old codes are now merely the prefixes: 26610 for Kérkyra Town and the centre of the island, 26630 for northern Corfu, 26620 for the far south and 26510 for Paxí.

Foreign visitors with tri-band mobiles can roam on one of the four Greek networks, but charges (despite intra-EU capping) remain extortionate. If you are staying more than a week or two, it makes sense to buy a local SIM with some talk-time included. It must be registered at time of purchase, but the number remains valid for a year from each top-up.

TIME ZONES

Greek time is GMT + 2. Greece observes Daylight Savings along with the rest of Europe (but not the USA), moving clocks one hour forward between the last Sunday in March and the last one in October.

In August, here is the time in the following cities:

New York	London	**Corfu**	Jo'burg	Sydney	Auckland
5am	10am	**noon**	11am	8pm	9pm

TOILETS

Public conveniences are best avoided. But if you are desperate in Kérkyra Town, there are toilets at the following locations: Platía I. Theotóki, near the Spianáda bandstand, on Platía Sarókko and at Platía Spiliás near the Old Port. Take along your own toilet paper. You should leave a small tip (up to €0.50) if there's someone in attendance.

You are always expected to put toilet tissue in the waste bin rather than down the toilet. Due to their narrow-bore drainage pipes, older toilets easily become clogged.

Where are the toilets?	**Pou íne i toualéttes?**

TOURIST INFORMATION

The Greek National Tourist Organisation, or Ellinikós Organismós Tourismoú (EOT; www.visitgreece.gr) has the following offices abroad, fine for general info and glossy pamphlets, but short on material specific to Corfu:

Australia: 37–49 Pitt Street, Sydney, NSW; 2000; tel: (2) 9241 1663.
UK and Ireland: 4 Conduit Street, London W1R 0DJ; tel: (020) 7495 9300.
US: 305 East 47th Street, New York, NY 10017; tel: (212) 421 5777.

The island's tourist information office in Kérkyra Town is a small, green, wooden kiosk halfway up the side of Platía Sarókko (daily 9am–5pm in season) – though information is limited to a useful town plan and basic leaflets.

TRANSPORT

Buses (*leoforía*). Unfortunately, the island's public bus service is not always efficient, but looking on the bright side, it is good value. Timetables are displayed at bus stops (**ΣΤΑΣΙΣ** – *stásis*) in the capital. There are no all-night bus services. There are two types of buses on the island. The blue urban buses serve towns and villages in the vicinity of Kérkyra Town, including Benítses, Kondókali, Gouviá, Dassiá, the Achilleion and Pélekas. Buses for Kanóni depart from near the Spianáda. All other blue buses leave from San Rocco Square (tel: 26610 31595). Long-distance buses are green-and-cream-coloured, but with variations for adverts; they leave from the coach station on Avramíou Street, by the New Fort (tel: 26610 39985). There is a designated website for bus services (www.ktelkerkyras.gr), however so far with no English version; for now obtain information from www.corfunet.com/corfu/transport/green_bus.php.

For all buses, buy your tickets on board or from kiosks in the square. You should only flag buses down at designated stops or other safe places, with a verge.

Taxis. Taxis based in Kérkyra Town are dark blue; those based in the country are grey. Taxi ranks in town are at the New Port, Old Port, Esplanade and San Rocco Square. There are meter tariffs: a slow one used within Kérkyra Town, and a fast rate for single out-of-town trips

What's the fare to…?   Póso éhi éna isitírio giá…?
When's the next bus to…?   Póte févgi to epómeno
                             leoforío giá…?

or between midnight and 6am (the meter is changed from 'slow' to 'fast' at the town boundary). Check upon getting into the cab; if the meter is mysteriously 'broken', you will have to agree on a fare with the driver. Radio taxis can be summoned (tel: 26610 33811, www.ctts.gr) for a small surcharge; an advance appointment for a set time has a bigger surcharge.

Ferries. Regular ferries run (in midsummer only) to Kefaloniá, and to Paxí via Igoumenítsa. But the Ionian islands are not a group for island-hopping: it takes three hours to sail to Paxí and seven hours to Kefaloniá. To get to any other islands requires changing on the mainland, at Pátra. Ferries also go to various ports in Italy. All depart from Kérkyra Town, though there is an additional service to Igoumenítsa from Lefkímmi (near Kávos) – useful for drivers as it's cheaper.

For current ferry schedules and fares check with authorised travel agents or the port authority tel: 26610 32655.

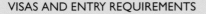

VISAS AND ENTRY REQUIREMENTS

European Union (EU) citizens may enter Greece for an unlimited length of time as long as they have a valid identity card or passport. Citizens of the US, Canada, Australia and New Zealand can stay for up to 90 days within any 180-day period upon production of a valid passport; no advance visas are needed. South African citizens require a Schengen Visa, applied for in advance at a Greek embassy or consulate.

There are no limits on the amount of hard currency visitors can import or export, though amounts in excess of 10,000 euros equivalent should be declared.

All goods brought into Greece from within the EU must have duty paid on them. There are no limitations on the amount of duty-paid goods that can be brought into the country.

W

WATER

Tap water is not drinkable in much of the island: it comes from well bores which may have been tainted by the sea (*glyfó* is Greek for brackish, a word you'll hear a lot). Known potable ones are in the square at Benítses, along the waterfront at Garítsa, and on Platía Políti at the top of Guilford in Kérkyra Town. The few springs high in the hills are usually okay to collect from.

WEBSITES AND INTERNET ACCESS

Internet Cafés. Internet access is available in almost every beach resort, if only through Wi-Fi zones. In Kérkyra Town try Netoikos at Kaloherétou 12–14, just off Kapodistríou.

Many Corfu travel agencies and other commercial enterprises have their own websites, which vary greatly in quality. Two of the best, and more heavily used, ones are **www.agni.gr** (with lively forums) and **www.kassiopi.com**. Other useful sites include:

www.terrakerkyra.gr Good overview site, with history, festivals, destinations.

http://thecorfiotmagazine.com/archive.html Back issues of the now-defunct monthly to download.

www.corfuwhatson.com/whatson Events calendar, by month.

http://corfublues.blogspot.com Excellent blog by local aficionado and scholar Jim Potts.

Y

YOUTH HOSTELS

The enormous Pink Palace at Ágios Górdis (slogan: 'People to Meet, Things to Do') is the island's backpacker hostel, hosting multinational crowds in both doubles and multi-bed rooms. Full information from www.thepinkpalace.com.

Recommended Hotels

The price categories below are for an en-suite double room (but without breakfast, typically €6–12 extra, unless otherwise stated) in high season. All hotel rates include VAT (Value Added Tax) and local taxes. In every room you'll find an official price placard on the back of the door. You should never pay more than this, and except at the busiest seasons – Easter week and August – the price ought to be significantly less.

Most of these hotels appear on generic booking websites, and have their own site (often with web discounts). All listed hotels accept credit cards, and provide air conditioning unless otherwise stated. Hotels in beach resorts are open only from late April/early May to September/October. Those in Kérkyra Town are open all year round.

Dialling from outside Greece, precede hotel numbers with the international country code +30.

€€€€€	over 200 euros
€€€€	150–200 euros
€€€	100–150 euros
€€	65–100 euros
€	below 65 euros

KERKYRA TOWN

Arkadion €€€ *Kapodistríou 44, Kérkyra Town, tel: 26610 30104, www.arcadionhotel.com.* Dead-central 3-star hotel overlooking the Spianáda, four minutes' walk from most museums. Rooms – side-facing ones a bit quieter – are spacious, with wrought-iron bedsteads, marble and wood furniture and beige floor tiles. Common areas include a tiny mezzanine lounge and equally compact first-floor breakfast salon, as well as a roof terrace that's a prime venue for watching the Easter events. 55 rooms.

Bella Venezia €€€ *N. Zambéli 4, Kérkyra Town, tel: 26610 46500, www.bellaveneziahotel.com.* Kérkyra Town's worst-kept secret, and enduringly popular, this 2008-renovated hotel occupies a converted neo-Classical former girls' school at the edge of Pórta Remoúnda district. The best rooms, with high ceilings and sometimes balconies, are on the first two storeys, though the third-floor suites can accommodate families of four. Breakfast is offered in the back-garden conservatory. Stylish lobby bar and helpful staff complete the picture. 31 rooms.

Cavalieri €€€€ *Kapodistríou St. 4, Kérkyra Town, tel: 26610 39041, www.cavalieri-hotel.com.* This converted six-storey 17th-century mansion, just off the Spianáda, offers an assortment of standard rooms and galleried suites (which can fit three at a pinch), though some are on the small and dark side. Worth a visit by non guests just to enjoy its roof garden's great views while nursing a drink. 50 rooms.

Corfu Palace Hotel €€€€€ *Dimokratías 2, Kérkyra Town, tel: 26610 39485, www.corfupalace.com.* The dowager empress of town hotels, a favourite with conferences and business folk as well as holiday-makers, this 5-star outfit scores for its unbeatable position just 10 minutes' walk from the Listón, and willing staff, as much for its accommodation. Standard rooms are large, with new soft furnishings and veneer floors, while superior units have better livery and double sinks in the bathrooms; all units have sea views over Garítsa Bay. Breakfast is taken indoors or out on the lawn garden by the saltwater pool. There's also an indoor pool by the small spa, and the island's only casino. 115 rooms.

Hermes € *Gerasímou Markorá 14–16, Pórto Reále area, tel: 26610 39268, www.hermes-hotel.gr.* Thoroughly overhauled in 2008, the Hermes is the best of the budget-option crop where Corfu Town is concerned, and accordingly this place is much in demand. Decor over two floors of high-ceilinged rooms is in pleasant taste, with light-hued veneer floors and solid-wood Asian furniture, and there are thoughtful touches such as mini sound systems and double glazing. Common areas are limited to a pleasant breakfast salon. 33 rooms.

Konstantinoupolis €€ *Zavitsiánou 11, Old Port, tel: 26610 48716, www.konstantinoupolis.com.gr.* Renovated building dating from 1862, but still pleasantly old-fashioned, this 2-star hotel has both sea and mountain views from the front balconied rooms, which are large – though bathrooms are small and basic, if brightly tiled. Rooms are reached either by a spiral wooden staircase or antique lift, past the more modern mezzanine breakfast area and lounge. 31 rooms.

THE SOUTH

Apollo Palace €€€ *Mesongí, tel: 26610 75433, www.apollopalace-corfu.com.* This attractive, well-designed complex set in 11 acres of gardens is popular with German, Belgian and east European families. Units, some shaded by olive trees remaining from the former grove here, are large and furnished to a decent standard, with beamed ceilings and terracotta tiles underfoot. Most patrons are on half-board or all-inclusive basis. Recent promotion to 5-star category is based on extensive common areas (including two pools, multiple restaurants, tennis court) and evening entertainment. 235 rooms. Open April–October.

Aquis Sandy Beach €€€ *Ágios Geórgios Argyrádon, tel: 26620 52145, www.aquisresorts.com* We generally don't recommend all-inclusive-only resorts, but this one is a cut above most such, with abundant and varied meal offerings, helpful staff and a roll-onto-the-beach setting. The 4-star complex is so vast that guests and their luggage are ferried by golf cart to some of the remoter units. It's probably better for families and the elderly than romantic couples, however. 562 rooms and apartments. Open early May–late Oct.

Avra € *Benítses, in new village, 400m south of square, 50m inland, tel: 26610 71111, www.hotelavracorfu.com.* Friendly little inn that's a firm favourite with those traversing the Corfu Trail, not least for the sake of the helpful English owners Andy and Sarah-Jane. Breakfast available downstairs in the fireplace lounge. Simple rooms are all varied, with antique floor tiles and fridges; 'budget' rooms lack balconies and air con. 16 rooms. Open Easter–Oct.

Boukari Beach € *Boúkari, 4km (2.5 miles) beyond Mesongí, tel: 26620 51791, www.boukaribeach.gr.* Some 700m/yds from the excellent, eponymous waterside restaurant *(see page 108)* are two peaceful, secluded units (inside Villa Lucia) sleeping up to four in each, as well as studios and double rooms in the larger Hotel Penelope, with all amenities including coffee machines. Villa Alexandra, next to the restaurant, is similar to Villa Lucia inside but with a hillside position has even more fantastic views. Open Apr–Oct.

Delfinia €€–€€€ *Moraïtika, tel: 26610 76320, www.delfiniahotels. gr.* The main hotel wing of the Delfinia and a further choice of low-rise annexes all stand behind a private pebble beach, set in a shady olive grove and lawns pleasantly studded with cypresses, palms and citrus trees. Here you'll find all the public amenities you'd expect to warrant the 4-star rating, though balconied rooms themselves are a bit on the spartan side. Rates are B&B. 185 rooms. Open late Apr–late Oct.

NORTH OF KERKYRA TOWN

Casa Lucia €€–€€€ *depending on cottage. Sgómbou hamlet, at Km 12 of Kérkyra–Paleokastrítsa road, tel: 26610 91419, www.casa-lucia-corfu.com.* A restored olive-mill complex set among lovingly tended gardens with a large pool. Just 8 self-catering units ranging from studios to family cottages; all share simple (read, 1980s vintage) if adequate furnishings, and are often occupied by patrons attending the yoga, t'ai chi or massage workshops held here. Peaceful setting at the very centre of the island makes this an excellent touring base. No on-site restaurant per se, but the affiliated *Bio-Bistro Lucciola* (often with entertainment) is just a few steps away on the main road. Open year round, but Nov–Mar on weekly or monthly basis.

Chandris Corfu/Dassiá €€€€ *Dassiá Bay, tel: 26610 97100, www. chandris.gr.* The Greek Chandris chain operates these two large hotels side by side on Dassiá Bay, separated from the sea by terraced private gardens. Rooms are in the main wings or in bungalows. The Dassiá – the first one you meet coming from Kérkyra Town – was completely gutted and renovated over the winter of 2010–11, and is now rated 5-star; the Chandris Corfu remains 4-star. Both are family-friendly and have all the facilities expected for their rating, including disabled access. Corfu Chandris 277 rooms; Dassiá Chandris 251 rooms. Open May–Oct.

Corfu Imperial €€€€€ *Komméno, tel: 26610 88400, www.grecotel. gr.* Set at the tip of a private peninsula with man-made sandy-cove beaches on the sheltered inland side, this luxurious hotel is considered one of the two or three top lodgings on the island – and thus often booked out. This self-contained resort has a huge seawater swimming pool, water sports, a choice of restaurants and bars, a tennis club, spa and gym. Rooms are luxuriously furnished and are either in the main block or in bungalows dotted around the pretty grounds with Italianate gardens and olive trees. 306 rooms, suites and villas. Open Apr–Oct.

Kontokali Bay €€€€–€€€€€ *Kondókali, tel: 26610 99000, www. kontokalibay.com.* This low-rise bungalow-style 'resort and spa' has most units scattered in clusters through beautiful gardens next to a private sandy beach. Superior standards (redone 2007–08) are like junior suites with their sofas and big balconies, while the gardenview family bungalows were renovated in 2010. Bathrooms have butler sinks and proper shower screens. Facilities are commensurate with a 5-star rating, and include an elevated infinity pool, beachside restaurant, state-of-the-art freestanding spa, tennis courts, water sports at the private port and an imaginative children's club. 152 rooms and suites, 81 bungalows, in several grades. Rates B&B; half board available. Open late Apr–Oct.

Nefeli €€ *Dafníla cove, beyond Komméno, tel: 26610 91033, www. hotelnefeli.com.* Small hotel in mock neo-Classical style, spread over three buildings among picturesque olive groves. Several 'design' rooms have wall murals; suites have rather 'hot' colour schemes. On-site pool, though it's just an 800-metre walk to the beach. 45 rooms and suites. Open May–Oct.

THE NORTHEAST

Nissaki Beach €€€€ *Nisáki, tel: 26630 91232, www.nissakibeach. gr.* This high-rise brutalist structure won't win any beauty contests, but once inside the Nissaki Beach it barely matters as the setting is one of the finest on Corfu, gazing across the bay in the direction of town. On the slight downside, not all the rooms are sea-view – 'oblique side view' would be a more accurate description – and beginning to show their age, while the pebbly beach itself is not brilliant – but there are ample sports facilities and a medium-sized pool just inland. The 4-star hotel is pitched at families, and priced on a half-board or all-inclusive basis. 233 rooms and 6 suites. Open Apr–Oct.

The White House €€€€ *Kalámi, tel: 26630 91040, www.corfu-kalami.gr.* The ground floor of the famous White House, where Lawrence Durrell wrote *Prospero's Cell,* is now a taverna with a rather chequered record. The upstairs has been converted into an airy self-catering holiday villa sleeping up to eight people, with a kitchen, two bathrooms, four bedrooms and with the original dining table and desk that Durrell used kept in situ. The location (at the very end of the road in Kalámi) and views – across the bay and beach and out to Albania – are splendid. Entire house by the week only. The same management keeps four other nearby apartment complexes.

THE NORTH AND NORTHWEST

Delfino Blu €€€€–€€€€€ *Ágios Stéfanos Gýrou, tel: 26630 51629, www.delfinoblu.gr.* This small boutique hotel has a gorgeous setting overlooking one of the best sandy beaches in the area, and is often full, even in spring or autumn. The self-catering units, decorated in pastel hues, all have sea views, balconies and mod cons. Gourmet restaurant downstairs and excellent pool and beach bars. On-site motor-yacht rental, plus small gym and sauna. 12 apartments and 3 suites. Open May–Oct.

Erikousa €€ *Eríkousa islet, tel: 26630 71110, www.hotelerikousa.gr.* The only bona-fide hotel on the smallest of the Diapóndia islets, near the village beach, and thus very popular all season – you'll probably have to book the preceding winter. Sea-view rooms are simple but tastefully done, plus there's a very competent in-house taverna – luckily, as there's little other choice here for eating out. Rates B&B. Open May–Sept.

Villa de Loulia €€€€ *Perouládes, 500m (545 yards) from Longás beach, tel: 26630 95394, www.villadeloulia.gr.* One of Corfu's few rural restoration inns, this mansion dating from 1803 has been refurbished to provide varying rooms, with high-standard furnishings and fittings in excellent taste. The bar, lounge and gourmet restaurant occupy a separate purpose-built structure flanking the large pool. Heating but only fans, no air conditioning. You're paying for the exclusivity – better value out of peak season. 9 rooms. Open May–Oct.

THE WEST

Akrotiri Beach Hotel €€€ *standard doubles* **€€€€€** *superior units Paleokastrítsa, tel: 26630 41237, www.akrotiri-beach.com.* The unique selling point of this modern, 4-star resort popular with package patrons – sister property to Kérkyra Town's Bella Venezia – is indisputably its setting on a headland overlooking the sea. The rooms, all sea view, are offered in three grades; decor in the standards is ripe for refreshing, however the east-facing superiors (some of them interconnecting) have benefited from a recent refit and sport veneer floors, pastel trim and showers with proper partitions. Common facilities include a medium-sized infinity pool with a normally priced restaurant, an indoor restaurant, free tennis court and independent dive centre by the public beach, and a private pebble beach. 127 rooms. Open May–Oct.

Fundana Villas €€ *Turn at Km 17 of Kérkyra–Paleokastrítsa onto 2km (1.2-mile) side road, tel: 26630 22532, www.fundanavillas.com.* Another 1980s restoration inn, this time converted from an 18th-century manor, with a commanding ridgetop position in the middle of a gorgeous landscape. Units, from double studios to family-sized bungalows or suites, are all different, some with brick-and-flagstone floors or timber beams, and recently refreshed. Large pool, bar and grill, olive-press museum on site. Active types can follow part of the Corfu Trail, which passes right by. 3 studios, 7 bungalows, 2 suites. Open Easter–Oct.

The Golden Fox €€ *Lákones, tel: 26630 49101, www.corfugolden fox.com.* Set on a slope above Paleokastrítsa, this small, family-run hotel has one of the most stunning locations on Corfu, with fantastic views overlooking the bays and islets below. Units are a mix of self-catering and not, double or twin beds. The complex includes a good restaurant, bar and pool, all with the same beautiful views, plus a shop selling a range of local embroidery, lace and textiles. Many guests return year after year. 11 rooms. Open May–Oct.

Levant Hotel €€ *Above Pélekas (fork right at the church), right beside 'Kaiser's Throne', tel: 26610 94230.* The Levant Hotel was constructed in 1989 in mock-traditional style, with the benefit of superb panoramic views both east and west over the island. Rooms are wood-floored, baths marble-trimmed. There's a medium-sized pool and spa tub on a grassy terrace, but with some of the island's best beaches a few kilometres away, you may not use them. Ground-floor faux-rustic common areas comprise wood and marble-floored bar and restaurant, with the breakfast area outside taking advantage of the view. Understandably, a popular wedding venue. 25 rooms. Open Apr–Oct.

PAXI

Paxos Club €€€€ *In an olive grove 1km (.6 miles) west of Gáios, tel: 26620 32450, www.paxosclub.gr.* This stylish small apart-hotel has been sensitively built around an 1896-vintage traditional island house, now converted to the restaurant for breakfast or dinner. There's a saltwater pool, a piano bar and children's playground. Choose between studios with pool or garden view, or garden family apartments fitting up to four people. 26 apartments. Open May–Sept.

Paxos Beach €€€€ *1.5km (1 mile) east of Gáios, tel: 26620 32211, www.paxosbeachhotel.gr.* This bungalow hotel comprised of stone-clad units that come in several grades leads down to a pebbly, very sheltered beach; if for any reason this doesn't suit, there's a magnificent large pool just behind. Ongoing renovations have dealt with superior seaview units and the common areas, with the lower-category accommodation to receive attention in 2012–13. 40 units. Open May–Sept.

INDEX

Berlitz pocket guide

Corfu

Seventh Edition 2012

Written by Donna Daily
Updated by Marc Dubin
Edited by Alexia Georgiou
Series Editor: Tom Stainer
Production: Tynan Dean, Linton Donaldson and Rebeka Ellam

Photography credits
AKG Images 15; Elizabeth Boleman-Herring 41, 50; Corbis 89; Kevin Cummins/APA 1, 2TR, 2MC, 3CR 3BR, 4BL, 4BR, 4TL, 4/5B, 5BC, 8, 13, 18, 23, 24, 26, 28, 31, 32, 33, 34, 38, 40, 47, 49, 53, 54, 56, 57, 64, 67, 69, 70, 73, 75, 82, 84, 85, 91, 93, 95; Britta Jaschinski/APA 4TL, 5MC, 5TC, 98, 100, 102; Paul Murphy 17, 36, 37, 58, 60, 63; iStockphoto 2TL, 3TL, 5TL, 71, 77, 81, 87, 96; Fotolia 3TR, 11. 78, 79; Topham Picturepoint 20; Phil Wood 43; Donna Dailey 44.

Cover picture: 4Corners Images

No part of this book may be reproduced, stored in a retrieval system or transmitted in any form or means electronic, mechanical, photocopying, recording or otherwise, without prior written permission from Berlitz Publishing. Brief text quotations with use of photographs are exempted for book review purposes only.

All Rights Reserved
© 2012 Apa Publications (UK) Limited

Printed in China by CTPS

Berlitz Trademark Reg. U.S. Patent Office and other countries. Marca Registrada. Used under licence from the Berlitz Investment Corporation

Every effort has been made to provide accurate information in this publication, but changes are inevitable. The publisher cannot be responsible for any resulting loss, inconvenience or injury.

Contact us

At Berlitz we strive to keep our guides as accurate and up to date as possible, but if you find anything that has changed, or if you have any suggestions on ways to improve this guide, then we would be delighted to hear from you.

Berlitz Publishing, PO Box 7910, London SE1 1WE, England.
email: berlitz@apaguide.co.uk
www.berlitzpublishing.com